Salad Menus

Great Meals in Minutes was created by Rebus Inc., and
published by Time-Life Books.

This edition published 1994 by Bloomsbury Books, an
imprint of The Godfrey Cave Group, 42 Bloomsbury Street,
London, WC1B 3QJ.

© 1994 Time-Life Books BV.

ISBN 1 85471 576 3

Printed and bound in Great Britain.

Salad Menus

Bruce Aidells
Menu 1
Calamari Vinaigrette	8
Asparagus Wrapped in Prosciutto	
Mushroom, Provolone, and Radish Salad	

Menu 2
Chinese Egg Vermicelli with Vegetables and Ham	10
Cold Beef Salad with Ginger Dressing	

Menu 3
Meat and Vegetable Salad	13
Creole-style Potato Salad with Sausage	
Lettuce and Tomatoes with Blue Cheese	

Jane Uetz
Menu 1
Consommé Madrilène	18
Lobster and Fruit Salad with Tarragon-Sherry Mayonnaise	
Whole-Wheat Muffins with Chives	

Menu 2
Cream of Winter Vegetable Soup	20
Warm Lentil and Sausage Salad	
Green Beans and Red Pepper Strips in Mustard Vinaigrette	

Menu 3
Stuffed Eggs Tapénade	23
Cherry Tomato and Melon Salad with Smoked Ham	
Fried Goat Cheese with Garlic Bread	

Mary Carroll Dremann
Menu 1
Oriental Chicken, Vegetable, and Noodle Salad	28

Menu 2
Curried Broccoli Salad with Pitta Toasts	30
Cucumber Raita	

Menu 3
Vegetarian Chef's Salad with Creamy Miso-Ginger Dressing	33
Savoury Herb and Cheese Muffins	

Victoria Wise
Menu 1
Fresh Tuna Niçoise	38
French Bread with Feta Cheese and Olive Oil	

Menu 2
Smoked Ham with Fresh Spinach Salad with Creamy Mustard Mayonnaise	40
Deep-fried Onion Rings	

Menu 3
Shrimp and Pasta with Spinach Pesto	42
Italian Bread with Garlic, Thyme, and Olive Oil	

Connie Handa Moore
Menu 1
Peasant-style Miso Soup	46
Ham, Vegetable, and Noodle Salad	
Strawberries with Frosted Sponge Fingers	

Menu 2
Shrimp and Vegetable Rice	48
Japanese Orange Mousse	

Menu 3
Glazed Beef and Mushrooms with Shredded Cabbage	51
Baked Tomato Pudding	

Susan Huberman
Menu 1
Crudités with Cavier Dip	56
Crabmeat and Mushroom Salad	

Menu 2
Roasted Peppers with Mozzarella and Sun-Dried Tomatoes	57
Pasta and Vegetables with Genoa Salami	
Pear, Watercress, and Belgian Endive Salad	

Menu 3
Warm Duck Salad with Mango Chutney	59
Rice with Pecans and Mint	
Orange and Radish Salad with Cinnamon	

Bloomsbury Books
London

Bruce Aidells

Menu 1
(*right*)
Calamari Vinaigrette
Asparagus Wrapped in Prosciutto
Mushroom, Provolone, and Radish Salad

Bruce Aidells is an enthusiastic cook who describes his food as substantial and lavishly seasoned, often with a generous amount of garlic. He likes to experiment with Italian, Chinese, and Louisiana Creole recipes, creating menus that are colourful as well as flavourful. He finds that serving two or three salads in one meal is a good way to mix and match tastes and textures, while providing nutritional balance.

The three cold salads of Menu 1 were inspired by his memories of meals he ate from the *antipasti* carts in Italy. Like most Italian dishes, these salads do not require elaborate garnishing to be appealing. A crusty loaf of Italian or French bread is all that is needed to complete this springtime lunch or dinner.

For the Chinese-style salads of Menu 2, Bruce Aidells combines vegetables and flavourings common to Chinese cooking with meats popular in this country. Both salads are adaptable. For example, the cook suggests substituting Chinese barbecued pork (*char su*), if you can find it, for the smoked ham in the vermicelli salad. And lean pork or dark-meat chicken or turkey can be used in the beef salad.

Inspired by French, English, Spanish, African, and native American cuisines, Menu 3 features a hot potato salad spiced with Creole mustard and Louisiana *andouille* sausage. With it, the cook serves a salad of cold meat and vegetables, and another consisting of lettuce and tomato wedges tossed with a blue cheese and anchovy dressing.

Elegant prosciutto-wrapped asparagus spears, topped with a shallot and mustard dressing, accompany chilled calamari vinaigrette. For this informal meal, serve the sliced mushrooms, radishes, and provolone cheese on individual salad plates.

Calamari Vinaigrette
Asparagus Wrapped in Prosciutto
Mushroom, Provolone, and Radish Salad

Squid (*calamari* in Italian) is available in many parts of the country. Although fresh squid is not sold live, it should look moist, have creamy white flesh partially covered with a patchy mauve membrane, and no sour or fishy odour. Most often squid is sold in frozen blocks. To thaw it, place the frozen squid in its original wrapping in a deep pan in the refigerator. It should be ready to cook in about 24 hours. For the *calamari* vinaigrette, the squid is blanched quickly and then marinated in a mildly seasoned dressing.

Proscuitto is an Italian-style dry-cured unsmoked ham, usually eaten raw. Top-quality prosciutto is deep pink, moist, and not too salty. If it is not available, substitute Wetphalian ham. Select smooth-skinned asparagus that are plump and bright green, with compact tips; open, leafy tips are a sure sign of age. Round, thick spears are usually more tender than thin or flat ones. Before storing the asparagus, cut a small piece from the bottom of each spear, then stand the spears upright in a container of cold water in the refrigerator. They should stay fresh for several days.

What to drink
In Italy, bright acidic dishes like these would be well matched with an equally bright acidic white wine like Pinot Grigio, or with a more supple, accomodating one like Soave.

Start-to-Finish Steps
1 Peel and mince garlic for calamari, asparagus, and mushroom salad recipes. Peel and finely chop shallots for asparagus recipe. Wash and dry parsley, and fresh herbs if using. Finely chop enough parsley to measure 60 g (2 oz) for calamari, asparagus, and mushroom salad recipes. Finely chop enough oregano to measure 15 g ($^1/_2$ oz) for calamari recipe and enough oregano or other herb to measure 2 tablespoons for mushroom salad recipe.
2 Follow calamari recipe steps 1 to 11.
3 Follow mushroom salad recipe steps 1 to 4.
4 Follow asparagus recipe steps 1 to 4 and mushroom salad recipe steps 5 to 7.
5 Follow asparagus recipe steps 5 to 7, mushroom salad recipe step 8, and serve with calamari.

Calamari Vinaigrette

1 tablespoon salt
1 Kg (2 lb) small squid
2 small red bell peppers
Small green bell pepper
2 scallions
Small red onion
30 g (1 oz) finely chopped parsley

Vinaigrette:
2 lemons
1 level tablespoon minced garlic
2 teaspoons salt
1 teaspoon freshly ground black pepper
15 g ($^1/_2$ oz) finely chopped fresh oregano, or 1 tablespoon dried
250 ml (8 fl oz) olive oil

1 In large saucepan, combine 4 ltrs (6 pts) water and 1 tablespoon salt and bring to a boil over high heat.
2 Meanwhile, fill large bowl half full with ice water.
3 Halve squid lengthwise and remove quill-like piece located at top of body sac. Rinse squid thoroughly under cold running water and cut each half lengthwise into 2 strips.
4 Plunge squid into boiling water for 20 seconds, or just until opaque. Immediately turn into colander and transfer to bowl of ice water; set aside.
5 Wash and dry red and green bell peppers. Core, halve, seed, and quarter peppers. Cut each quarter crosswise into 20 cm (8 inch) wide strips; set aside in medium-size bowl.
6 Wash scallions and dry with paper towels. Trim off ends and discard. Chop scallions finely and place in bowl with peppers.
7 Halve onion, reserving one half for another use. Peel and finely dice remaining half; add to bowl. Add chopped parsley and set aside.
8 Squeeze enough lemon juice to measure 4 tablespoons.
9 Turn chilled squid into colander to drain; dry with paper towels. Rinse and dry large bowl.
10 For vinaigrette, combine lemon juice, garlic, salt, pepper, oregano, and oil in large bowl and beat with fork until blended.
11 Add squid and chopped ingredients to vinaigrette and toss until evenly coated. Cover bowl with plastic wrap and refrigerate until ready to serve.

Asparagus Wrapped in Prosciutto

2 teaspoons salt
12 large asparagus spears (about 500 g (1 lb) total weight)
12 thin slices prosciutto (about 1 Kg (2 lb) total weight)
½ teaspoon minced garlic
2 level tablespoons finely chopped shallots
2 tablespoons raspberry vinegar, preferably, or red wine vinegar
1 level tablespoon Dijon mustard
2 level tablespoons finely chopped parsley
6 tablespoons olive oil

1   Combine 1¼ ltrs (2 pts) water and salt in large skillet and bring to a boil over high heat.
2   Meanwhile, snap off tough woody bottoms of asparagus. Peel stalks, if desired, and rinse under cold running water.
3   Add asparagus to boiling water in a single layer. Cover skillet and cook about 6 minutes, or just until asparagus are tender when pricked with point of a knife.
4   Turn cooked asparagus into colander and immediately refresh under cold running water; set aside to drain.
5   Pat asparagus dry with paper towels. Wrap each spear from stem to just below tip with a slice of prosciutto. Divide asparagus among 4 dinner plates; set aside.
6   For dressing, combine garlic, shallots, vinegar, mustard, and parsley in small bowl. Whisking continuously, add olive oil in a slow, steady stream and stir until dressing is well blended and creamy.
7   Spoon dressing over asparagus and serve.

Mushroom, Provolone, and Radish Salad

250 g (8 oz) mushrooms
1 bunch red radishes
125 g (4 oz) provolone cheese
2 level tablespoons finely chopped parsley
1 level tablespoon Dijon mustard
2 tablespoons red wine vinegar
Pinch of sugar
1 teaspoon minced garlic
2 level tablespoons finely chopped fresh oregano, basil, marjoram or chervil, or 2 teaspoons dried
6 tablespoons olive oil
4 tablespoons sour cream or crème fraîche

1   Wipe mushrooms clean with damp paper towels. Slice thinly and place in large bowl.
2   Wash radishes under cold running water and dry with paper towels. Slice thinly to measure about 175 g (6 oz) and add to bowl with mushrooms.
3   Cut cheese into 5 cm (2 inch) long by 3 mm (⅛ inch) strips and add to sliced vegetables.
4   Add parsley to bowl with vegetables and cheese and toss to combine. Cover with plastic wrap and refrigerate until ready to serve.
5   For dressing, combine mustard, vinegar, sugar, garlic, and herbs in food processor or blender, and process briefly to combine.
6   With machine running, add oil in a slow, steady stream, and process until thick and creamy, scraping down sides of container as necessary.
7   With machine off, add sour cream or crème fraîche. Turn machine on and off until ingredients are blended; set aside.
8   Pour dressing over vegetables and cheese and toss until evenly coated. Divide among 4 salad plates and serve.

Chinese Egg Vermicelli with Vegetables and Ham
Cold Beef Salad with Ginger Dressing

The vermicelli salad includes three ingredients often used in Chinese cooking – Chinese egg noodles, snow peas, and dried black mushrooms. The snow peas should be crisp and bright green, with the tiny peas just visible inside. To store the pods, refrigerate them unwashed in a perforated plastic bag; they will last four to five days. If you must use frozen snow peas, blanch them just until they are heated through; otherwise, they become soggy.

Two chilled salads – vermicelli with vegetables and ham, and beef with ginger dressing – make an impressive buffet lunch or supper. For an authentic touch, offer your guests the option of using chopsticks.

Dried Chinese black mushrooms have a characteristic meaty flavour. They are sold by weight in cellophane packets wherever Oriental foods are available.

What to drink
Try a slightly sweet light German wine such as a Riesling *Kabinett* from the Moselle or the Rhine. Or serve a Chinese or Japanese beer.

Start-to-Finish Steps
1   Follow vermicelli salad recipe steps 1 to 10.
2   Follow beef salad recipe steps 1 to 8.
3   Follow vermicelli salad recipe steps 11 to 13.
4   Follow beef salad recipe step 9 and serve with vermicelli salad.

Chinese Egg Vermicelli with Vegetables and Ham

10 dried Chinese black mushrooms (about 30 g (1 oz) total weight)
500 g (1 lb) fresh Chinese egg vermicelli, or 250 g (8 oz) dried vermicelli
Salt
125 g (4 oz) snow peas
125 g (4 oz) smoked ham, sliced
1 bunch coriander
125 g (4 oz) fresh mung beansprouts
1 tablespoon peanut oil
2 eggs
2 teaspoons sugar
2 tablespoons Chinese black vinegar or white wine vinegar
1 tablespoon light soy sauce
6 tablespoons Oriental sesame oil

1   For mushrooms, bring 250 ml (8 fl oz) water to a boil in tea kettle. For vermicelli, combine 4½ ltrs (8 pts) water and 1 tablespoon salt in stockpot and bring to a boil over high heat.

2   In small bowl, combine dried mushrooms with 1 cup boiling water and set aside.

3   For snow peas, bring 1¼ ltrs (2 pts) water and 1 tablespoon salt to a boil in medium-size saucepan over high heat.

4   Meanwhile, cut ham into 5 cm (2 inch) long by 5 mm (¼ inch) wide strips; set aside.

5   Plunge snow peas into boiling water in saucepan and blanch 30 seconds. Turn into colander and refresh under cold running water; drain. Dry and set aside.

6   Wash and dry coriander. Trim off stems and discard. Coarsely chop coriander; set aside.

7   Place sprouts in colander, rinse under cold running water, and drain. Dry sprouts and set aside.

8   Add vermicelli to boiling water in stockpot and cook 1 minute for fresh, or according to package insructions for dried. Transfer vermicelli to large strainer and refresh under cold running water; set aside to drain.

9   In medium-size skillet, heat peanut oil over medium high heat.

10 Meanwhile, using fork, beat eggs in small bowl until blended. Add to skillet and cook about 3 minutes per side, or until firm. Carefully slip omelette out onto plate in one piece; set aside. Rinse and dry bowl.

11 Drain mushrooms and rinse under cold water. Using kitchen scissors, cut off stems and discard. Cut mushrooms into 5 mm (¼ inch) wide strips. Cut omelette into 1 cm (½ inch) wide strips; set aside.

12 For dressing, combine sugar, vinegar, and soy sauce in small bowl. Whisking vigorously, gradually add sesame oil and stir until blended.

13 In large serving bowl or on platter, combine vermicelli, snow peas, mushrooms, ham, sprouts, half the coriander, and toss to combine. Pour dressing over salad and toss until evenly coated. Arrange omelette strips around salad and sprinkle with remaining coriander.

pieces and cut celery on diagonal into very thin slices. Add celery to boiling water and blanch 2 minutes. Then add scallions and blanch another 15 seconds. Transfer vegetables to colander and refresh under cold running water; drain. Pat dry with paper towels.

8 In shallow serving bowl or on platter, combine beef, red bell pepper, celery, and scallions, and toss to combine.

9 Whisk dressing to recombine. Pour dressing over salad and toss until evenly coated. sprinkle with toasted sesame seeds and serve.

Added touch

For this simple dessert, select berries that are bright red and plump, with no tinges of white or green.

Cold Beef Salad with Ginger Dressing

2 level tablespoons sesame seeds
2 cloves garlic
2.5 cm (1 inch) piece fresh ginger
1 level tablespoon sugar
1 tablespoon rice or white wine vinegar
1 tablespoon light soy sauce
1 tablespoon Oriental sesame oil
1 tablespoon peanut oil
750 g (1½ lb) rare roast beef, thinly sliced
Small red bell pepper
1 level tablespoon salt
3 bunches scallions
2 stalks celery

1 In small heavy-gauge skillet, toast sesame seeds over medium heat, stirring constantly to prevent scorching, 2 minutes, or until lightly browned and fragrant. Transfer to plate and set aside to cool.

2 Peel and mince garlic. Peel and mince enough ginger to measure 2 teaspoons.

3 Combine garlic, ginger, sugar, vinegar, and soy sauce in small bowl. Whisking continuously, gradually add sesame and peanut oil and stir until blended; set aside.

4 Cut roast beef into 5 mm (¼ inch) wide strips.

5 Wash and dry red bell pepper. Halve, core, and seed pepper. Cut into 5 mm (¼ inch) strips; set aside.

6 Combine 1¼ ltrs (2 pts) water with salt in medium-size saucepan and bring to a boil over high heat.

7 Meanwhile, trim off ends from scallions and celery and discard. Cut scallions into 7.5 cm (3 inch) long

Sweet-and-Sour Strawberries

500 g (1 lb) strawberries
2 level tablespoons granulated sugar
1 tablespoon raspberry vinegar
250 ml (8 fl oz) sour cream
2 level tablespoons brown sugar

1 Gently rinse strawberries under cold running water and dry. Hull berries and halve lengthwise.

2 Combine granulated sugar and vinegar in large bowl and stir with fork until blended. Add berries and toss until evenly coated. Set aside for at least 30 minutes.

3 Divide berries among 4 bowls and top each serving with a heaping tablespoon of sour cream. sprinkle with brown sugar and serve.

Meat and Vegetable Salad
Creole-style Potato Salad with Sausage
Lettuce and Tomatoes with Blue Cheese

Creole-style potatoes and sausage go well with a light meat and vegetable salad and with lettuce and tomatoes.

This three-salad menu is good throughout the year and can be altered to use what you have on hand. For instance, in the cold meat salad you can use lean pork or ham, chicken, or dark-meat turkey. If asparagus is not in season, you can use broccoli, green beans, or cauliflower instead. If you prefer a vegetarian salad, omit the meat.

The hot potato salad is very spicy; for a milder version, reduce the amount of hot pepper sauce and Cayenne. The Louisiana *andouille* sausage used in this recipe imparts a distinctive smoky flavour. Unlike French *andouille*, this American version is made with pork meat rather than intestines. It is highly seasoned with garlic and Cayenne pepper before being smoked. You can substitute Polish *kielbasa* or Portuguese *linguiça* sausages, but these lack the intense flavour of *andouille*. The salad dressing contains Creole mustard, a pungent coarse-grained brown mustard that sometimes includes horseradish. Look for it in speciality food shops.

What to drink
A robust white wine such as an Alsatian Sylvaner or Pinot Blanc or an earthy red Côtes du Rhône or California Zinfandel would go nicely with the flavours of these dishes.

13

Start-to-Finish Steps

1 Wash scallions and dry with paper towels. Trim off ends and discard. Mince enough scallions to measure 100 g (3 oz) for potato salad recipe and coarsely chop enough to measure 45 g (1½ oz) for meat and vegetable salad recipe; set aside.
2 Follow potato salad recipe steps 1 to 3.
3 While potatoes are cooking, follow meat and vegetable salad recipe steps 1 to 10.
4 Follow potato salad recipe step 4 and lettuce salad recipe steps 1 to 3.
5 Follow potato salad recipe steps 5 to 10.
6 Follow meat and vegetable salad recipe steps 11 and 12, and rinse and dry food processor or blender.
7 Follow lettuce salad recipe steps 4 to 6.
8 Follow potato salad recipe steps 11 and 12, and serve with meat and vegetable salad and lettuce salad.

Meat and Vegetable Salad

Salt
500 g (1 lb) green beans
175 g (6 oz) cherry tomatoes
30 g (1 oz) sliced almonds
250 g (8 oz) cooked pork, chicken, or turkey
2 lemons
2 teaspoons Dijon mustard
Large egg
125 ml (4 fl oz) peanut oil
125 ml (4 fl oz) olive oil
Freshly ground black pepper
45 g (1½ oz) coarsely chopped scallions

1 Preheat oven to 180°C (350°F or Mark 4).
2 Combine 2½ ltrs (4 pts) water and 2 tablespoons salt in medium-size saucepan and bring to a boil over high heat.
3 Meanwhile, trim off ends of beans and discard. Cut beans in half.
4 Wash, dry, and halve cherry tomatoes; set aside.
5 Add beans to boiling water and cook 3 to 5 minutes, or until crisp-tender.
6 While beans are cooking, arrange almonds on baking sheet in a single layer and place in oven, shaking pan occasionally to prevent scorching, 5 to 8 minutes, or until lightly toasted.
7 Cut meat into 1 cm (½ inch) dice; set aside.
8 Turn beans into colander and refresh under cold running water; set aside to drain.
9 Squeeze enough lemon juice to measure 4 tablespoons.
10 Remove almonds from oven and set aside to cool.
11 For dressing, combine lemon juice, mustard, and egg in food processor or blender and process just until blended. With machine running, gradually add peanut oil and olive oil in a slow, steady stream and process until thick and creamy. Add salt and pepper to taste.
12 Combine meat, beans, tomatoes, and scallions, and half the toasted almonds in large serving bowl. Add just enough dressing to bind salad and toss to combine. Reserve remaining dressing for another use. Sprinkle salad with remaining almonds and set aside until ready to serve.

Creole-style Potato Salad with Sausage

Salt
1 Kg (2 lb) small red boiling potatoes
Small red onion
100 g (3 oz) minced scallions
15 g (¹/₂ oz) minced parsley
6 tablespoons cider vinegar
4 leaves lettuce (optional)
6 tablespoons olive oil
250 g (8 oz) Louisiana andouille, linguiça, or kielbasa
  sausage
1 clove garlic, minced
1 level tablespoon Creole or Dijon mustard
¹/₄ teaspoon Cayenne pepper
¹/₂ teaspoon freshly ground black pepper
Hot pepper sauce

1 In medium-size saucepan, bring 2¹/₂ ltrs (4 pts) water, 1 level tablespoon salt, and potatoes to a boil over high heat.
2 While water is coming to a boil, peel and mince enough red onion to measure 60 g (2 oz); set aside.
3 When water comes to a boil, partially cover pot, reduce heat to medium-high, and cook potatoes 20 to 30 minutes, or until they can be pierced easily with tip of a sharp knife.
4 When potatoes are cooked, turn into colander to drain and set aside to cool.
5 When potatoes are cool enough to handle, cut each in half and then into 5 mm (¹/₄ inch) thick slices.
6 Combine potatoes, onion, scallions, and parsley in large bowl and sprinkle with 3 tablespoons cider vinegar.
7 Line serving platter with lettuce, if using.
8 Heat olive oil in medium-size skillet over medium heat.
9 Coarsely chop sausage. Add sausage to skillet and sauté, stirring, 3 minutes, or just until it begins to brown.
10 Remove pan from heat and, with slotted spoon, transfer sausage to paper towels to drain. Add sausage to vegetables.
11 To fat remaining in pan, add garlic, mustard, Cayenne, remaining 3 tablespoons vinegar, pepper, and hot pepper sauce to taste and bring to a boil, whisking continuously, over medium-high heat.
12 Pour hot vinaigrette over salad and toss gently to combine. Turn out onto platter and serve immediately.

Lettuce and Tomatoes with Blue Cheese and Anchovy Dressing

1 head lettuce
2 medium-size tomatoes
125 g (4 oz) blue cheese
1 clove garlic, peeled
4 anchovy fillets
1 level tablespoon Dijon mustard
2 tablespoons red wine vinegar
1 level tablespoon dried oregano
6 tablespoons olive oil

1 Wash and dry lettuce. Tear leaves into quarters. Wrap in paper towels and refrigerate until ready to serve.
2 Wash and dry tomatoes. Core each tomato and cut into wedges; set aside.
3 Crumble enough cheese into small pieces to measure 30 g (1 oz); set aside.
4 For dressing, combine garlic, anchovy fillets, mustard, vinegar, and oregano in food procesor or blender and process just until paste-like.
5 With machine running, add olive oil in a slow, steady stream and process until mixture is creamy.
6 In large salad bowl, combine lettuce and tomato wedges. Pour dressing over salad and toss until evenly coated. Sprinkle with cheese and set aside until ready to serve.

Leftover suggestion
Reheat leftover Creole potato salad by sautéing it briefly until the potatoes and onions turn crisp and brown. When served with a tossed green salad, it makes a substantial luncheon.

Jane Uetz

Menu 1
(*Right*)
Consommé Madrilène
Lobster and Fruit Salad with
Tarragon-Sherry Mayonnaise
Whole-Wheat Muffins with Chives

When planning her meals, whether formal or informal, Jane Uetz likes to inject a surprise element that generally elicits comments from her guests. Often it is an unusual combination of ingredients. For example, in her rich Menu 1 salad, adapted from a dish she onced sampled in the Spanish Pavilion restaurant at the New York World's Fair, she arranges sliced fruits around chunks of fresh lobster dressed with an unusual tarragon and sherry-flavoured mayonnaise. The salad is preceded by consommé Madrilène, a tomato soup that may be served hot or chilled, and whole-wheat muffins with chives.

The height-of-summer salad in Menu 3 combines cherry tomatoes and melon balls – an unexpected tart-sweet mix – with slices of ham. The cook also offers hard-boiled eggs stuffed with tapénade – a paste of capers, anchovies, garlic, egg yolks, and lemon juice. The word tapénade derives from the Provençal *tapéno*, meaning capers, a traditional ingredient in this popular spread.

For the warm salad of Menu 2, Jane Uetz pairs lentils (often bland when served alone) and highly spiced Spanish *chorizo* sausage, and binds them with a tangy vinaigrette. A creamy vegetable soup made from cauliflower, carrots, onion, and celery tempers the sausage, and a second salad of green beans and red pepper strips adds colour and texture.

Fresh flowers set a festive tone for this sumptuous meal. Garnish each mug of consommé with a slice of lemon and a sprig of coriander if you like, and offer a basket of muffins hot from the oven. The lobster and fruit salad, with its creamy mayonnaise dressing, is arranged on a bed of red leaf lettuce.

Consommé Madrilène
Lobster and Fruit Salad with Tarragon-Sherry Mayonnaise
Whole-Wheat Muffins with Chives

Lobster turns any meal into a feast. Buy live lobsters that are very active in the tank. You will need a lobster steamer or a stockpot large enough to accommodate two lobsters. Once the salted water boils, rinse the lobsters briefly under cold water, then plunge them in to the pot. To test for doneness, remove each lobster from the cooking water with tongs and pull off one small leg; the lobster is fully cooked when the leg comes off readily.

What to drink
A full-bodied white wine is nice with this meal. Good choices would be a California Chardonnay or a white Burgundy such as Mâcon or Saint-Véran.

Start-to-Finish Steps
1 Wash coriander, chives, and fresh tarragon if using, and dry with paper towels. Reserve 4 sprigs coriander for garnish, if desired, and chop enough of remainder to measure 1 tablespoon for consommé recipe. Snip enough chives to measure 15 g (¹/₂ oz) for muffin recipe. Chop enough tarragon to measure 1 teaspoon for salad recipe. Juice 1¹/₂ lemons for salad recipe, and cut 4 slices from remaining lemon half for consommé garnish, if desired.
2 Follow salad recipe steps 1 to 7.
3 While lobster is cooling, follow consommé recipe steps 1 to 4.
4 Follow salad recipe steps 8 and 9.
5 Follow muffin recipe steps 1 to 6.
6 Follow consommé recipe steps 5 to 7.
7 Follow muffin recipe step 7, and serve with consommé as first course.
8 Follow salad recipe steps 10 and 11 and serve.

Consommé Madriléne

1 Kg (2 lb) very ripe fresh tomatoes, or 1 kg (2 lb) can plum tomatoes
1 tablespoon chopped fresh coriander, plus 4 sprigs for garnish (optional)
1 ltr (1³/₄ pts) chicken stock
4 lemon slices for garnish (optional)

1 If using fresh tomatoes, bring 2¹/₂ ltrs (4 pts) of water to a boil in medium-size saucepan over high heat.
2 Plunge tomatoes into boiling water and blanch 30 seconds. Turn tomatoes into colander and refresh under cold running water. Peel, quarter, and remove seeds. If using canned tomatoes, drain, quarter, and remove seeds.
3 In medium-size saucepan, combine tomatoes, chopped coriander, and stock, and bring to a boil over high heat. Reduce heat to medium, cover pan, and simmer 15 minutes.
4 Remove soup from heat, uncover pan and set aside to cool.
5 Transfer soup to food processor or blender and purée. If using processor, purée soup in batches.
6 Return soup to saucepan and heat through over medium heat.
7 Divide soup among 4 mugs or bowls and garnish each serving with a slice of lemon and a sprig of coriander, if desired.

Lobster and Fruit Salad with Tarragon-Sherry Mayonnaise

Salt
100 ml (3 fl oz) mayonnaise
3 level tablespoons heavy cream
3 level tablespoons ketchup
2 tablespoons dry sherry
1 teaspoon chopped fresh tarragon, or $1/2$ teaspoon dried
Two 1-$1^1/2$ Kg (2-$2^1/2$ lb) lobsters, or two 250 g (8 oz) packages frozen lobster tails, cooked according to package directions
Medium-size red bell pepper
1 orange
Juice of $1^1/2$ lemons
1 ripe pear
1 head red leaf lettuce
1 large banana

1 In large stockpot, bring $1^1/4$ ltrs (2 pts) salted water to a boil over high heat.
2 Meanwhile, combine mayonnaise, heavy cream, ketchup, sherry, and tarragon in small bowl, stirring until well blended. Cover dressing with plastic wrap and set aside.
3 Add lobsters to boiling water head first, cover pot, and cook over high heat 15 minutes.
4 Meanwhile, wash bell pepper and dry with paper towel. Halve, core, and seed pepper. Cut into 5 mm ($1/4$ inch) wide strips; set aside.
5 Peel orange, removing as much white pith as possible. Cut crosswise into 5 mm ($1/4$ inch) thick rounds; set aside.
6 In small bowl, combine 2 tablespoons lemon juice and 500 ml (1 pt) cold water. Halve pear and cut lengthwise into 6 mm ($1/4$ inch) thick slices. Add pear slices to lemon water to prevent discolouration; set aside.
7 With tongs, transfer lobsters to colander and set aside to cool.
8 Wash lettuce and dry with paper towels. Remove and discard any bruised or discoloured leaves. Line serving platter with lettuce, cover with plastic wrap, and refrigerate until ready to serve.
9 When lobsters are completely cool, remove meat from shells, using nutcracker to crack claws. Discard shells. Cut meat into bite-size pieces and place in large bowl.
10 Peel banana and cut on diagonal into 3.5 cm ($1^1/2$ inch) slices. Place banana in small bowl and sprinkle with remaining lemon juice. Toss slices to coat evenly.
11 Spoon lobster into centre of lettuce-lined platter and arrange fruit slices and pepper strips around it. Drizzle some mayonnaise over lobster and serve remaining mayonnaise on the side.

Whole-Wheat Muffins with Chives

125 g (4 oz) plain flour
125 g (4 oz) whole-wheat flour
3 teaspoons baking powder
1 teaspoon salt
60 g (2 oz) shortening (not oil)
250 ml (8 fl oz) milk
15 g ($1/2$ oz) snipped chives

1 Preheat oven to 230°C (450°F or Mark 8).
2 Grease 12-cup muffin pan or cup-cake tray.
3 In medium-size bowl, combine plain and whole-wheat flour, baking powder, and salt, and stir with fork to blend.
4 Cut in shortening with pastry blender or 2 knives until the mixture resembles coarse cornmeal
5 With your fist, make a well in the centre of the flour mixture. Add milk and chives, and, using a fork, stir just enough to moisten dry ingredients.
6 Fill each cup of muffin pan half full with batter and bake 12 to 15 minutes, or until muffins are golden.
7 Transfer muffins to napkin-lined basket and serve hot.

Added touch
Serve this spread of pugnent Roquefort cheese, Armagnac, and orange-flavoured liqueur at room temperature for easier spreading and fuller flavour.

Armagnac Cheese Spread

125 g (4 oz) Roquefort cheese
125 g (4 oz) cream cheese
125 g (4 oz) unsalted butter
2 tablespoons Armagnac
$1^1/2$ teaspoons orange liqueur, such as Grand Marnier or Cointreau
30 g (1 oz) chopped walnuts
Water biscuits or other unsalted crackers

1 Allow cheeses and butter to soften at room temperature.
2 Using electric mixer, blend cheeses with butter in medium-size bowl until creamy.
3 Still beating, gradually add Armagnac and orange liqueur, and beat until mixture is smooth.
4 Stir in walnuts. Serve the spread with crisp crackers.

Cream of Winter Vegetable Soup
Warm Lentil and Sausage Salad
Green Beans and Red Pepper Strips in Mustard Vinaigrette

The main-course salad features lentils and *chorizo* sausage. The lentils should be washed before use to remove any tiny pebbles, but they do not require pre-soaking. Spanish *chorizo* is a pork sausage highly spiced with Cayenne and garlic. Some *chorizos* are sold fresh, but most are dried and smoked. Use the dried type for this recipe. *Chorizo* is available in some supermarkets and at delicatessens. You can substitute a hard salami, such as Genoa, or pepperoni, but because they are even more garlicky than *chorizo*, eliminate the garlic from the dresing.

For a filling dinner on a cold winter's night, serve steaming bowls of vegetable soup topped with sour cream and parsley, lentil and sausage salad with a red-wine vinegar dressing, and green beans with red pepper strips.

What to drink

Serve your guests a full-flavoured Zinfandel, a Châteauneuf-du-Pape, or an Italian Dolcetto with these dishes. Or you can follow the cook's suggestion for an amber English beer or ale.

Start-to-Finish Steps

1 Peel and chop enough onion to measure 60 g (2 oz) each for soup and salad recipes. Wash and dry parsley; mince enough to measure 15 g (½ oz) each for salad and soup recipes.
2 Follow soup recipe steps 1 to 6.
3 While soup is simmering, follow salad recipe steps 1 through 4 and green beans recipe steps 1 to 7.
4 Follow salad recipe step 5 and soup recipe step 7.
5 Follow salad recipe steps 6 to 8.

6 Follow soup recipe steps 8 to 12.
7 Follow salad recipe step 9, soup recipe step 13, and serve with green beans.

Cream of Winter Vegetable Soup

Small head cauliflower (about 500 g (1 lb))
2 medium-size carrots
2 stalks celery
3 level tablespoons unsalted butter
60 g (2 oz) chopped yellow or white onion
1/4 teaspoon whole black peppercorns
1/2 teaspoon dried tarragon
1/2 bay leaf
1 ltr (1 3/4 pts) chicken stock
30 g (1 oz) flour
250 ml (8 fl oz) milk
Salt and freshly ground pepper
125 ml (4 fl oz) sour cream (optional)
15 g (1/2 oz) minced parsley

1 Rinse cauliflower. Cut into florets; set aside.
2 Peel carrots. Cut crosswise into 2.5 cm (1 inch) long pieces.
3 Wash celery and chop enough to measure 100 g (3 oz).
4 In large saucepan, heat 1 tablespoon butter over medium heat. Add onion and sauté, stirring occasionally, 5 minutes, or until onion is soft and translucent.
5 Meanwhile, prepare *bouquet garni* by making a small pouch from a double thickness of cheesecloth. Place peppercorns, tarragon, and 1/2 bay leaf in pouch, and tie securely with kitchen string.
6 Add half of the stock and *bouquet garni* to saucepan with onion, and bring to boil over high heat. Reduce heat to medium-low, cover pan, and simmer 30 minutes.
7 Remove *bouquet garni* and discard. Set pan of vegetables aside to cool slightly.
8 Transfer vegetables to food processor, or to a blender if you want a smoother texture, and purée. Return purée to saucepan; set aside.
9 In small saucepan, melt remaining 2 tablespoons

butter over medium-low heat. Whisk in flour and cook 1 minute.

10 Remove pan from heat. Whisking continuously, add milk in a slow, steady stream and stir until blended. Return pan to medium-high heat and bring to a boil.

11 Whisking continuously, add milk mixture to vegetable purée and stir until blended. Whisk in remaining stock.

12 Place soup over high heat and bring to a boil. Add salt and pepper to taste.

13 Divide soup among 4 bowls and garnish with sour cream and parsley, if desired.

Warm Lentil and Sausage Salad

250 g (8 oz) chorizo or other dried hot sausage
125 g (4 oz) brown lentils
60 g (2 oz) chopped yellow or white onion
1 teaspoon salt
1 bay leaf
1 bunch watercress
Small red onion for garnish
$^1/_4$ teaspoon minced garlic
2 tablespoons lemon juice
125 ml (4 fl oz) vegetable oil
2 tablespoons red wine vinegar
$^1/_4$ teaspoon ground cumin
$^1/_4$ teaspoon hot pepper sauce
15 g ($^1/_2$ oz) minced parsley

1   Remove casing from chorizo and cut sausage into 3.5 cm (1$^1/_2$ inch) long by 5 cm (2 inch) wide strips.

In small nonstick skillet, sauté chorizo about 5 minutes, or until lightly browned.

2   Rinse lentils in colander or large strainer; drain.

3   Transfer chorizo to paper towels to drain.

4   In large saucepan, combine lentils, onion, salt, bay leaf, and 1$^1/_4$ ltrs (2 pts) cold water, and bring to a boil over high heat. Reduce heat to medium, cover pan, and simmer gently 15 to 17 minutes, or until lentils are tender.

5   Drain lentils; discard bay leaf. Cover pan.

6   Wash and dry watercress. Trim stems and discard.

7   Peel red onion and cut into very thin slices.

8   For dressing, in small bowl, combine garlic, lemon juice, and remaining ingredients except parsley, and stir with fork until blended; set aside.

9   Just before serving, combine lentils and sausage in large bowl. Pour dressing over salad and toss. Divide salad among 4 dinner plates and sprinkle with parsley. Garnish with watercress and red onion slices, and serve.

Green Beans and Red Pepper Strips in Mustard Vinaigrette

500 g (1 lb) green beans
4 teaspoons salt
Large red bell pepper
$^1/_4$ teaspoon sugar
1 teaspoon balsamic vinegar
1$^1/_2$ tablespoons cider vinegar
2 teaspoons Pommery or other coarse-grained mustard
100 ml (3 fl oz) vegetable oil

1   Bring 500 ml (1 pt) of water to a boil in medium-size saucepan.

2   In colander, rinse beans in cold water and trim ends.

3   Add salt and beans to boiling water, cover pan, and cook 3 to 5 minutes, or just until beans are crisp-tender.

4   Wash and dry red pepper. Core, halve, and seed pepper. Cut lengthwise into thin strips.

5   For vinaigrette, combine sugar and remaining ingredients in small bowl and stir with fork until blended.

6   Turn beans into colander and refresh under cold water.

7   In medium-size serving bowl, combine beans and pepper strips. Pour vinaigrette over vegetables and toss.

Stuffed Eggs Tapénade
Cherry Tomato and Melon Salad with Smoked Ham
Fried Goat Cheese with Garlic Bread

Melon balls with cherry tomatoes and ham, goat cheese on garlic bread, and stuffed eggs are a colourful company meal.

The two types of melon and smoked ham make a delectable combination. To get a good cantaloupe, select one with smooth a depression at the stem end, indicating the melon was nearly ripe when picked; it will only need to stand a few days at room temperature to soften. When ripe, the cantaloupe will emit a distinctive aroma. Choose a honedew with a yellowish skin colour and slightly waxy or oily-looking surface. Sniff the stem end; a vine-ripened honeydew will have a sweet fragrance. A honeydew with hard, green-tinged skin was picked too early and will never achieve the full flavour of a vine-ripened melon. You can keep a honeydew at room temperature for a few days.

If you like, try other melons. Although the salad is best with fresh melon balls, you can use the frozen type as a winter substitute. If you cannot buy ham, substitute smoked turkey or salami.

For the fried goat cheese, use a log-shaped Montrachet without an ash coating. This French cheese is soft, moist, and has only a touch of the 'goatiness' associated with many goat cheeses. Montrachet is sold at most cheese or speciality food stores. It slices and fries best when very cold, so place it in the freezer for at least five minutes to firm it.

What to drink

This menu, with its bold flavours, demands a crisp white wine or a light red one. For a white, choose Sancerre Pouillt-Fumé, or Sauvignon Blanc; for a red, try a young Zinfandel or Gamay Beaujolais.

Start-to-Finish Steps

One hour ahead: Set eggs out to reach room temperature.

1 Peel and mince garlic for eggs recipe and cheese recipe. Wash parsley, and fresh herbs if using, and dry with paper towels. Reserve 8 sprigs of parsley for garnish, if using, for eggs recipe. Trim stems and mince enough parsley to measure 1 tablespoon for eggs recipe. Chop enough basil and snip enough chives to measure 1 tablespoon each for salad recipe. Squeeze enough lemon juice to measure 1 teaspoon for eggs recipe and 2 tablespoons for salad recipe.
2 Follow eggs recipe steps 1 and 2, and salad recipe steps 1 to 4.
3 Follow eggs recipe step 3 and cheese recipe steps 1 to 4.
4 Follow eggs recipe steps 4 to 7.
5 Follow salad recipe steps 5 and 6, cheese recipe steps 5 to 9, and serve with the eggs.

Stuffed Eggs Tapénade

4 large eggs, at room temperature
60 g (2 oz) jar capers
60 g (2 oz) tin anchovy fillets, or 1 tablespoon anchovy paste
1 clove garlic, minced
1 tablespoon minced parsley, plus 8 sprigs for garnish (optional)
1 teaspoon Dijon mustard
1 teaspoon lemon juice
1 tablespoon white wine vinegar
1 tablespoon olive oil

1 Place eggs in small saucepan and add enough cold water to cover by at least $2^1/_2$ cm (1 inch). Cover pan and bring water to a rapid boil over high heat.
2 When water reaches a rapid boil, turn off heat and let eggs sit on stove 15 minutes.
3 Fill medium-size bowl half full with cold water. Transfer eggs to cold water and set aside to cool.
4 Drain 1 teaspoon capers and mince. If using anchovy fillets, drain 3 fillets and mince.
5 In small bowl, combine capers, anchovies, garlic, minced parsley, mustard, lemon juice, vinegar, and oil, and stir with fork until blended.
6 Peel hard-boiled eggs and halve lengthwise. Add yolks to bowl and mash ingredients together with fork to form a smooth tapénade paste.
7 Fill whites with tapénade and divide stuffed eggs among 4 salad plates. Garnish plates with parsley sprigs, if desired.

Cherry Tomato and Melon Salad with Smoked Ham

175 g (6 oz) cherry tomatoes
Small cantaloupe
Small honeydew or other melon
100 ml (3 fl oz) olive oil
2 tablespoons lemon juice
$^1/_4$ teaspoon salt
1 to 2 level tablespoons chopped fresh basil, or $^1/_2$ to 1 teaspoon dried
1 to 2 level tablespoons snipped fresh or frozen chives
1 head red leaf lettuce
250 g (8 oz) thinly sliced smoked ham

1 Wash tomatoes and dry with paper towels. Halve tomatoes; set aside.
2 Halve cantaloupe and small honeydew melons; remove and discard seeds. Using large end of

melon baller, carefully scoop out enough flesh to measure about 750 g (1¹/₂ lb) of melon balls.

3   In large bowl, combine oil, lemon juice, salt, and 1 to 2 level tablespoons each of fresh basil and chives, depending on sweetness of melons.

4   Add melon balls and tomato halves to dressing in bowl; toss until evenly coated. Cover bowl and let stand 30 minutes at room temperature.

5   Wash lettuce and dry in salad spinner or with paper towels. Remove and discard any bruised or discoloured leaves. Divide lettuce among 4 large plates and top with melon and tomatoes.

6   Roll up each slice of ham; arrange slices around salad and serve.

Fried Goat Cheese with Garlic Bread

2 slices home-style white bread
¹/₄ teaspoon paprika
250 g (8 oz) log Montrachet cheese, well chilled
4 teaspoons unsalted butter, approximtely
1 tablespoon olive oil
1 clove garlic, minced
1 baguette (¹/₄ pound loaf)

1   Preheat oven to SLOW.

2   Trim crusts from white bread and discard; chop bread coarsely. Using food processor or blender, process bread into crumbs. You should have about 45 g (1¹/₂ oz).

3   In pie pan or shallow dish, combine bread crumbs and paprika.

4   Place cheese in freezer to chill at least 5 minutes.

5   Cut well-chilled cheese into eight 1 cm (¹/₂ inch) thick slices. Dip each cheese slice in breadcrumbs and press to help crumbs adhere.

6   In medium-size skillet, heat 2 tablespoons butter over medium-high heat. When butter stops foaming, add all of the cheese slices and fry 1 minute per side, or until lightly browned and cheese is warm and soft. Using slotted spatula, transfer cheese to heatproof platter and keep warm in oven.

7   Reduce heat under skillet to medium-low. Add remaining butter, olive oil, and garlic to skillet and sauté 1 minute.

8   Meanwhile, cut baguette on diagonal into eight 1 cm (¹/₂ inch) thick slices. Add bread slices to skillet and sauté, adding more butter, if necessary, 1 minute per side, or until lightly browned.

9   Transfer bread slices to serving platter and top with cheese.

Added touch

When melting the chocolate, be sure to include the shortening, or the chocolate will be too thick to coat the sherbet balls properly. The cook suggests using a Jaffa orange for the garnish, but any other type of orange will do.

Frosted Sherbet Balls

1¹/₄ ltrs (2 pts) orange sherbet
4 squares semi-sweet chocolate
2 tablespoons shortening (not oil)
1 Jaffa or other orange for garnish (optional)
4 fresh mint sprigs for garnish (optional)

1   Line a metal freezer tray with waxed paper or aluminium foil.

2   Using ice cream scoop, scoop sherbet into 8 balls and place on tray. Keep chilled in freezer.

3   Combine chocolate and shortening in top of double boiler and place over hot water, stirring occasionally, until chocolate melts.

4   Remove top of double boiler from hot water and set chocolate aside to cool slightly, about 3 minutes.

5   Remove sherbet balls from freezer. Drizzle each one with chocolate until coated and return to freezer.

6   Place 4 dessert plates in freezer to chill.

7   With sharp paring knife, peel orange, if using, removing as much white pith as possible. Segment orange.

8   Wash mint sprigs, if using, and dry with paper towel.

9   Divide sherbet balls among chilled dessert plates and garnish each serving with orange sections and a mint sprig, if desired.

Mary Carroll Dremann

Menu 1
(*Left*)
Oriental Chicken, Vegetable,
and Noodle Salad

Like many of her fellow Californians, Mary Carroll Dremann loves to create bountiful salads using the local farm-fresh produce available on the West Coast year round. To the delight of her guests, she often goes beyond the standard salad markings and incorporates ethnic ingredients to achieve intriguing flavour combinations. For an exciting visual presentation, she likes to cut fruits and vegetables into various shapes. And to emphasize rather than obscure the natural flavour of each ingredient, she dresses the salads lightly.

The Oriental salad of Menu 1 has a sesame oil, *tamari*, and rice vinegar dressing flavoured with ginger, coriander, and honey, which is also used to baste the baked chicken breasts. This combination of seasonings brings out the sweetness of the chicken meat.

Menu 2 contrasts the taste of broccoli with the pungency of curry spices in the Indian-style salad. A tart *raita*, or yogurt condiment (here made with cucumber), and crisp toasted pitta triangles are the accompaniments. You can prepare both the salad and the *raita* up to two days in advance without spoiling their texture or flavour.

In menu 3, the vegetarian salad is composed of red and green pepper strips, tomato and egg wedges, and sprouts on a bed of brown rice. A mixture of fresh ginger, honey, and Japanese *miso* (soybean paste) is the dressing.

A woven tablecloth, dark wine glasses, and chopsticks add to the exotic mood of this one-dish meal. The chicken, vegetable, and noodle salad is carefully composed on a bed of leaf lettuce and garnished with fresh coriander.

Oriental Chicken, Vegetable, and Noodle Salad

For this Oriental salad, the cook uses a number of unusual ingredients, including *udon* or *soba* noodles, macadamia nuts, Japanese eggplants, and fresh *shiitake* mushrooms. Fresh *shiitake* have wide dark-brown caps and small woody stems. They should be firm and feel dry. Layered in a container and covered with damp cheesecloth or paper towels, they can be refrigerated for a week. These mushrooms are sold in many supermarkets.

Marble-sized macadamias, considered by many to be the world's finest nuts, are creamy white and slightly sweet. Because they are rich in oil, macadamias should be stored in the freezer.

Tiny Japanese eggplants, sold at quality greengrocers and some Oriental and Middle Eastern markets, are sweeter than Western varieties. They should be firm and have a rich, deep-purple colour. Any type of baby eggplant could be substituted.

Despite its name, *tamari* is virtually unknown in Japan. Because *tamari* is brewed with very little wheat, it tends to have a fuller, stronger taste than other soy sauces. This dark, unrefined soy is available in most health food stores.

What to drink

Tea, hot or iced, would accompany this dish perfectly. If you prefer wine with your meal, a good choice is a relatively full-bodied dry white California Chardonnay.

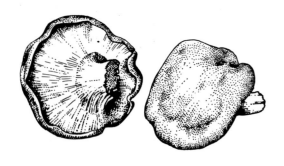

Shiitake mushrooms

Start-to-Finish Steps

1 Follow salad recipe steps 1 to 16.
2 While chicken is cooling, follow salad recipe steps 17 to 19.
3 Follow salad recipe steps 20 and 21 and serve.

Oriental Chicken, Vegetable, and Noodle Salad

Dressing:
Large clove garlic
5 cm (2 inch) piece fresh ginger
250 ml (8 fl oz) Oriental sesame oil
175 ml (6 fl oz) rice vinegar
175 ml (6 fl oz) tamari or other soy sauce
$1/2$ teaspoon ground coriander
2 level tablespoons honey

Salad:
2 skinless, boneless chicken breasts (about 750 g
    (1 $1/2$ lb) total weight), halved
250 g (8 oz) asparagus, or 2 small Japanese eggplants
2 tablespoons salt
Small bunch fresh coriander
125 g (4 oz) snow peas
200 g (7 oz) package Japanese udon or soba noodles
Small head leaf lettuce
Small head Belgian endive
2 large fresh shiitake mushrooms
1 tablespoon Oriental sesame oil
60 g (2 oz) macadamia nuts or almonds

1 Preheat oven to 180°C (350°F or Mark 4).
2 Peel and mince garlic. Peel and grate enough ginger to measure 2 heaped teaspoons.
3 In large bowl, combine sesame oil, vinegar, tamari, garlic, ginger, ground coriander, and honey. Whisk dressing until blended; set aside.
4 Lightly oil baking sheet.
5 Rinse chicken under cold running water and dry with paper towels. Place chicken breasts, smooth side up, on prepared baking sheet.
6 If using eggplants, rinse under cold running water and dry. Cut each eggplant lengthwise into quarters and place on baking sheet with chicken.
7 Liberally brush chicken and eggplant with dressing; reserve remaining dressing. Bake 30 minutes or

until juices run clear when chicken is pierced with the tip of a knife.

8   While chicken and eggplant are baking, fill stockpot or kettle two-thirds full with cold water, add the salt, and bring to a boil over high heat.

9   Meanwhile, wash fresh coriander and dry with paper towels. Finely chop enough coriander to measure 45 g (1½ oz) and set aside for garnish. Reserve remainder for another use.

10 Wash snow peas, and asparagus if using, under cold running water. Trim off ends of snow peas and discard. Break off tough woody bottoms of asparagus; peel stalks if desired.

11 Break noodles into thirds. Add to stockpot and boil 7 minutes.

12 While noodles are boiling, place snow peas in strainer and immerse in boiling noodle water for 30 seconds. Immediately refresh under cold running water, and turn onto paper towels to drain.

13 Repeat process for asparagus, but immerse 3 to 5 minutes, or until crisp-tender. Refresh under cold water and drain on paper towels.

14 Turn noodles into colander and drain. Transfer to large bowl with reserved dressing. Toss noodles gently until evenly coated and set aside.

15 Wash lettuce under cold running water and dry with paper towels. Remove and discard any bruised or discoloured leaves. Tear lettuce into bite-size pieces. Line 4 dinner plates with lettuce.

16 Remove chicken and eggplant from oven and set aside to cool slightly.

17 Meanwhile, rinse endive under cold water and dry with paper towel. Separate leaves; set aside.

18 Wash shiitake mushrooms under cold running water and dry with paper towel. Separate leaves; set aside.

19 In medium-size sauté pan, heat 1 tablespoon sesame oil over low heat. Add mushrooms and nuts, and sauté, stirring and tossing, 5 minutes, or until mushrooms are lightly browned and soft. Remove pan from heat; set aside.

20 When chicken is cool enough to handle, cut croswise into 5 mm (¼ inch) wide strips.

21 With slotted spoon, arrange equal portions of marinated noodles in centre of each lettuce-lined plate. Top one half of noodles with chicken slices and the other half with mushrooms and nuts. Arrange endive, snow peas, and asparagus spears or eggplant quarters around noodles, and pour remaining marinade over salad. Garnish with chopped coriander and serve immediately.

Added touch

These toasted slices of French bread with roasted vegetables supplement a salad meal. Let your guests assemble open-faced sandwiches: First, squeeze the cooked garlic out of its skin and spread it on the bread; then spread a layer of roasted eggplant over the garlic, and top with a piece of red pepper.

French Bread with Roasted Garlic Vegetables

6 tablespoons olive oil, approximately
2 Japanese eggplants
2 large red bell peppers
2 heads garlic
1 loaf French bread

1   Preheat oven to 180°C (350°F or Mark 4). Lighty oil a 30 cm (12 inch) x 22.5 cm (9 inch) baking sheet.

2   Wash eggplants under cold running water and dry with paper towls. Quarter each eggplant lengthwise and place on prepared baking sheet.

3   Wash bell peppers and dry with paper towels. halve, core, and seed peppers. Cut each half into quarters and place on baking sheet.

4   Trim off top fourth from garlic heads to expose the cloves. Place on baking sheet.

5   Brush vegetables liberally with olive oil and roast 30 minutes, or until peppers are limp and eggplant and garlic are slightly brown.

6   During the last 5 minutes of roasting, place loaf of French bread, unwrapped, in oven and heat.

7   Cut warm bread on diagonal into 5 cm (2 inch) thick slices. With spatula, divide vegetables equally among 4 plates and serve accompanied by bread.

Curried Broccoli Salad with Pitta Toasts
Cucumber Raita

A chilled salad of curried broccoli with toasted pitta bread triangles and cucumber raita are ideal hot-weather fare.

An Indian meal is considered incomplete without a dish made with yogurt, such as *raita*. A *raita* can be made with yogurt and any type of raw or cooked vegetables or fruit. This one, called *kheere ka raita*, uses a seedless cucumber. Choose a cucumber that is firm and green, without any soft or shriveled spots. Refrigerate it in the plastic wrap in which it is sold, and use it within a week. Hothouse cucumbers are longer than standard varieties, and because their smooth skin is unwaxed, they do not require peeling.

The cooking liquid for the broccoli calls for apple juice, which adds swetness to the curry and eliminates any bitter aftertaste from the spices. You can substitute cauliflower for the broccoli if you prefer; it will take on the yellow curry colour.

What to drink
The cook suggests a cold, light beer or iced tea as the best beverage with this Indian-style meal.

Start-to-Finish Steps
One hour ahead: Immerse frozen shrimp for salad recipe in bowl of cold water to thaw.

1 Follow salad recipe steps 1 to 14.
2 Follow raita recipe steps 1 to 5.
3 Follow salad recipe steps 15 to 17, and serve with chilled raita.

Curried Broccoli Salad with Pitta Toasts

2 heads broccoli
175 ml (6 fl oz) apple juice
Large onion
1 large clove garlic
Medium-size carrot
2.5 cm (1 inch) piece fresh ginger
4 large mushrooms (about 125 g (4 oz) total weight)
2 level tablespoons unsalted butter
1 tablespoon Oriental sesame oil
$^1/_2$ teaspoon caraway seeds
3 teaspoons ground turmeric
1 teaspoon ground coriander
1 teaspoon ground cardamom
$^1/_2$ teaspoon ground cumin
$^1/_2$ teaspoon cinnamon
$1^1/_2$ teaspoons yellow mustard seeds
1 teaspoon salt
1 teaspoon Cayenne pepper, approximately
250 g (8 oz) package frozen tiny shrimp, thawed
3 level tablespoons honey
60 g (2 oz) raw peanuts
4 round pitta breads

1 head lettuce
2 to 4 level tablespoons dried grated unsweetened coconut

1 Rinse broccoli under cold running water. Trim off stems and reserve for another use. Cut broccoli into florets. You should have about 750 g (1$^1/_2$ lb).

2 In medium-size saucepan, combine broccoli, apple juice, and 125 ml (4 fl oz) water, and bring to a boil over high heat.

3 Meanwhile, halve and peel onion. Cut one half crosswise into very thin slices. You will have about 100 g (3 oz). Reserve remaining half for another use. Peel and mince enough to measure 1 level tablespoon; set aside.

4 Cover broccoli, reduce heat to medium-low, and simmer gently about 5 minutes, or until crisp-tender.

5 While broccoli is cooking, peel and trim carrot. Halve crosswise, then cut each half lengthwise. Cut quarters into thin julienne; set aside.

6 Using coarse side of grater, grate enough unpeeled ginger to measure 1 level tablespoon.

7 Turn broccoli into colander or large strainer set over large bowl and immediately refresh under cold running water; reserve cooking liquid.

8 Wipe mushrooms with damp paper towels. Cut into thin slices; set aside.

9 Preheat oven to 130°C (250°F or Mark $^1/_2$).

10 In a large heavy-gauge skillet, melt butter over medium heat. Stir in sesame oil, caraway seeds, turmeric, coriander, cardamom, cumin, cinnamon, mustard seeds, salt, and Cayenne to taste. Cover skillet and heat until seeds begin to pop.

11 Stir in onion, ginger, and mushrooms, and sauté over medium-high heat about 1 minute, or until begins to soften but not brown.

12 Stir in garlic and carrot, and sauté another minute.

13 Add broccoli and cooking liquid and bring to boil over a high heat. Boil, uncovered, 2 minutes, or until liquid is reduced to 250 ml (8 fl oz). Rinse and dry bowl.

14 Remove skillet from heat. Stir in shrimp, honey, and peanuts. Turn salad into large dry bowl, cover, and chill.

15 With kitchen scissors, cut each pitta into quarters and arrange on baking sheet. Toast 10 minutes, or until crisp.

16 While pittas are toasting, wash lettuce and dry in salad spinner or with paper towels. Remove and discard any bruised or discoloured leaves. Divide among 4 dinner plates.

17 Remove salad from refrigerator. Divide among lettuce-lined plates and sprinkle with grated coconut to taste. Serve with toasted pitta.

Cucumber Raita

1 cucumber (about 350 g (12 oz))
500 ml (1 pt) plain yogurt
250 ml (8 fl oz) sour cream
2 teaspoons cumin seeds
2 teaspoons salt

1 Wash and dry cucumber. Halve unpeeled cucumber crosswise; reserve one half for another use.
2 Using coarse side of grater, grate half of cucumber and place in medium-size bowl.
3 Add yogurt and sour cream to cucumber and stir to combine.
4 In small nonstick heavy-guage skillet, toast cumin seeds over medium heat, shaking pan to avoid scorching, about 2 minutes, or until they release their fragrance. Stir in salt.
5 Add salted cumin seeds to yogurt mixture and stir to combine. Cover with plastic wrap and refrigerate raita until ready to serve.

Added touch
For a traditional accompaniment to the curried salad, serve currant and grape chutney. If the grapes are very sweet, you may want to use less honey; sample the chutney as it cooks and add honey to taste.

Sweet Currant and Green Grape Chutney

Medium-size clove garlic
5 cm (2 inch) piece fresh ginger
625 g (1¼ lb) seedless green grapes
175 ml (6 fl oz) apple juice
1 teaspoon cinnamon
1 teaspoon ground cardamom
125 g (4 oz) currants
175 g (6 oz) honey
175 g (6 oz) apple cider vinegar

1 Peel and mince enough garlic to measure 1 teaspoon. Using grater, grate enough unpeeled ginger to measure 2 tablespoons.
2 Rinse grapes under cold running water and drain; dry with paper towels. Remove grapes from stems.
3 Combine all ingredients in a small heavy-gauge saucepan and bring to a boil over high heat. Continue to boil mixture, uncovered, 5 minutes.
4 Remove pan from heat and set aside to cool slightly.
5 Purée mixture in two batches in food processor, or in blender.
6 Return chutney to saucepan and bring to a boil over high heat. Reduce heat and simmer 10 minutes.
7 Pour chutney into strainer set over medium-size bowl; do *not* press. Discard any liquid drained from chutney.
8 Turn chutney into small bowl and serve warm, or cover and chill in refrigerator before serving.

For a wholesome lunch or light dinner, serve this colourful meal-in-a-bowl with savoury cheese-enriched muffins.

This robust salad contains brown rice, an unmilled grain with its nutritive outer bran layer intact. Brown rice takes longer to cook than white rice, but it still retains a pleasant nutty taste. To avoid using two pots, boil the rice and eggs together. The rice sinks to the bottom of the pot, and when the eggs finish cooking, you can easily lift them out of the pot without disturbing the rice.

What to drink

A light semi-dry white wine would suit this menu well. A California French Colombard or a slightly sweet California Chenin Blanc would also be good.

Start-to-Finish Steps

About one-half hour ahead: Set out eggs for muffin recipe to come to room temperature.

1. Wash parsley for salad recipe, and fresh herbs if using for muffin recipe, and dry with paper towels. Mince enough parsley to measure 15 g (½ oz). Mince enough basil, marjoram, thyme, and dill to measure 2 level tablespoons each.
2. Follow salad recipe steps 1 and 2.
3. While eggs are cooking, follow muffin recipe steps 1 to 5.
4. Follow salad recipe steps 3 and 4.
5. While rice is cooking, follow muffin recipe steps 6 to 8.
6. While muffins are baking, follow salad recipe steps 5 to 13.
7. Follow muffin recipe step 9 and salad recipe step 14.
8. When muffins have cooled slightly, follow salad recipe step 15 and serve with muffins.

33

Vegetarian Chef's Salad with Creamy Miso-Ginger Dressing

300 g (10 oz) long- or short-grain brown rice
2 extra-large eggs
1 bunch scallions
4 large cloves
1 lemon
15 g (1/2 oz) minced parsley
3/4 teaspoon dry mustard
4 tablespoons apple cider vinegar
1/2 teaspoon salt
1/4 teaspoon freshly ground white pepper
4 tablespoons olive oil
4 tablespoons safflower oil
1 red bell pepper
1 green bell pepper
2 medium-size tomatoes (about 500 g (1 lb) total weight)
125 g (4 oz) mixed sprouts, such as alfalfa, mung bean, or soybean
60 g (2 oz) Parmesan cheese

Dressing:
2.5 cm (1 inch) piece fresh ginger
1 1/2 level tablespoons white miso paste
175 ml (6 fl oz) sesame or safflower oil
4 tablespoons raspberry or apple cider vinegar
3 tablespoons tamari or other soy sauce
1/4 teaspoon ground coriander
2 level tablespoons honey

1   In large heavy-gauge saucepan, combine rice and 1 ltr (1 3/4 pts) cold water and bring to a boil over medium-high heat.
2   Add eggs to boiling water; reduce heat to medium and cook, uncovered, 10 minutes.
3   Using slotted spoon, transfer eggs to colander and rinse under cold running water; set aside to cool.
4   Continue cooking rice, uncovered, another 10 minutes.
5   Check level of rice cooking liquid; it should be just even with level of rice. If not, add water. Cover pan, reduce heat to very low, and simmer very gently 25 more minutes until rice has absorbed liquid.
6   Meanwhile, wash and dry scallions. Mince scallions to measure about 60 g (2 oz); set aside. Peel and mince garlic. Squeeze enough lemon juice to measure 2 tablespoons.
7   Combine scallions, garlic, parsley, dry mustard, cider vinegar, lemon juice, salt, white pepper, olive oil, and safflower oil in large bowl, and whisk until blended; set aside.
8   Wash and dry bell peppers. Halve, core, and seed peppers. Reserve one half of each pepper for

another use. Cut remaining halves lengthwise into 5 mm (1/4 inch) wide strips.
9   Wash tomatoes and dry with paper towels. Core and halve tomatoes. Cut each half into quarters; set aside. Place sprouts in strainer, rinse, and set aside to drain.
10 In food processor fitted with steel blade or with grater, grate Parmesan; set aside. Rinse and dry processor bowl.
11 Using coarse side of grater, grate enough unpeeled ginger to measure 1 teaspoon for dressing.
12 In food processor or blender, combine miso, oil, vinegar, tamari, 3 tablespoons cold water, ginger, coriander, and honey, and process until thick and creamy; set aside.
13 Peel eggs and cut lengthwise into quarters; set aside.
14 When rice is cooked, turn into bowl with scallion mixture. Add Parmesan and toss to combine.
15 Turn warm rice into large salad bowl. Top with tomatoes, sprouts, pepper strips, and egg quarters. Pour creamy dressing over salad and serve.

Savoury Herb and Cheese Muffins

350 g (12 oz) cheddar cheese
2 level tablespoons unsalted butter
250 g (8 oz) plain flour, plus flour for dusting pan
3 teaspoons baking powder
1/2 teaspoon salt
4 extra-large eggs, at room temperature
250 ml (8 fl oz) buttermilk
2 level tablespoons honey
2 level tablespoons each minced fresh basil, dill, marjaram, and thyme, or 1 tablespoon each dried

1   Preheat oven to 200°C (400°F or Mark 6).
2   Using food processor fitted with shredding disc, or grater, shred cheese; set aside.
3   In small heavy-gauge saucepan, melt butter over low heat.
4   Lightly oil a 12-cup muffin or cup-cake pan and dust with flour.
5   Sift flour, baking powder, and salt into large bowl; set aside
6   In medium-size bowl, combine eggs and buttermilk, and whisking until frothy. Add melted butter and honey, and whisk briefly to combine.
7   Fold wet ingredients into dry ingredients. Add herbs and cheese, and stir just until blended; do *not* overmix.

8 Spoon batter into prepared muffin pan, filling each cup two-thirds full, and bake 20 to 25 minutes, or until muffins are lightly browned and springy to the touch.

9 Turn muffins out onto rack and let cool before serving.

Added touches

These piquant, bite-sized hors d'oeuvres are easy to prepare. The marinated hearts keep for up to two weeks in the refrigerator.

Baked Artichoke Hearts

4 medium-size artichokes
3 level tablespoons cream cheese
3 level tablespoons freshly grated Parmesan cheese
175 ml (6 fl oz) safflower or olive oil
100 ml (3 fl oz) raspberry vinegar or red wine vinegar
1 level tablespoon minced fresh oregano, or 1 teaspoon dried
2 level tablespoons minced fresh basil, or 2 teaspoons dried

1 In large stockpot, bring 7 ltrs (12 pts) water to a boil.

2 While water is coming to a boil, rinse artichokes lengthwise.

3 Place cream cheese in small bowl and set aside to soften. Place Parmesan on flat plate; set aside.

4 Add artichokes to boiling water and boil 10 minutes.

5 Using tongs, transfer artichokes to colander and set aside to cool slightly.

6 Meanwhile, combine oil, vinegar, and herbs in medium-size bowl; set aside.

7 When artichokes are cool enough to handle, trim stems, cut back leaves halfway, and remove hairy choke; discard stems and leaves. Add artichoke hearts to oil and vinegar, and marinate 30 minutes.

8 Preheat oven to 180°C (350°F or Mark 4).

9 Lightly oil baking sheet.

10 Remove artichokes from marinade and drain. Spread cut sides of each quarter with 1/2 teaspoon cream cheese, roll in Parmesan, and place on prepared baking sheet.

11 Bake artichokes 10 to 12 minutes. Serve hot.

This frothy mousse of puréed fresh berries contains tangy fresh lemon juice and sweet maple syrup. For an even more refreshing dessert, chill the glasses.

Lemon-Berry Mousse

3 medium-size lemons
350 g (12 oz) strawberries or raspberries
2 large eggs
3 level tablespoons arrowroot or cornstarch
175 ml (6 fl oz) maple syrup
250 ml (8 fl oz) heavy cream
1/2 teaspoon vanilla extract
1/4 teaspoon ground cardamom
1 whole nutmeg

1 Place bowl for whipping cream in freezer to chill.

2 Rinse and dry 2 lemons. Using zester or grater, remove enough rind to measure 2 level tablespoons.

3 Squeeze enough lemon juice to measure 125 ml (4 fl oz).

4 Rinse berries under cold running water and dry. If using strawberries, remove stems and discard.

5 In food processor or blender, purée 175 g (6 oz) of berries; set aside.

6 Separate eggs, placing yolks in small heavy-gauge saucepan and whites in large bowl; set aside whites.

7 Add arrowroot or cornstarch, lemon juice, lemon rind, and maple syrup to yolks, and whisk until blended. Whisk in puréed berries.

8 Whisking vigorously, heat berry mixture over low heat, 5 to 6 minutes, or until mixture has reached the consistency of pudding.

9 Turn mixture into stainless-steel bowl, cover, and place in freezer to chill 10 minutes.

10 Rinse and dry mint sprigs, if using; set aside.

11 Beat egg whites with electric mixer until stiff. Rinse beaters in cold water; chill in freezer about 5 minutes.

12 Place heavy cream in chilled bowl and beat with electric mixer at high speed until stiff. Gently stir in vanilla and cardamom.

13 Using rubber spatula, fold whites into whipped cream.

14 Remove berry mixture from freezer and gently fold into whipped cream mixture. Cover and return bowl to freezer for at least 1 hour before serving.

15 If using strawberries, thinly slice all but 4 of the remaining berries and line bottoms of 4 parfait glasses or large goblets with sliced berries. If using raspberries, reserve 4 berries for garnish and place an equal portion of whole berries in bottom of each dessert glass. Divide mousse among glasses and top each serving with 1 whole berry and grating of nutmeg.

Victoria Wise

Menu 1

(*Left*)

Fresh Tuna Niçoise
French Bread with Feta Cheese
and Olive Oil

Victoria Wise spent her childhood in Japan and later lived in the south of France, where she apprenticed in a charcuterie – the French version of a butcher shop. This diverse background has influenced her cooking and menu planning: She uses classic French cooking techniques, yet handles her ingredients with a characteristic Oriental lightness.

Today, Victoria Wise lives in California, where she often creates salads with vegetables from her own garden. The ham, spinach, and potato salad of Menu 2 is perfect for an early autumn luncheon, when spinach is just up and new red potatoes are ready to be dug. She mixes the spinach with slices of smoked ham, but you can also make the salad with any mild smoked meat, such as pork loin, chicken. or turkey. When new red potatoes are out of season, use waxy white potatoes or colourful sweet potatoes.

In menu 1 she offers fresh tuna Niçoise – a salad reminiscent of her days in provence. Niçoise dishes are usually garnished with anchovies and black olives, and this salad is no exception. It is best when the basic ingredients _ tomatoes, green beans, and sweet basil – are in season.

The shrimp and *fusilli* (corkscrew pasta) salad of Menu 3 is in keeping with the trend towards using pasta in any form. She dresses the salad with a pesto sauce made with fresh spinach as well as basil. Garlic bread is the accompaniment.

An oval earthenware platter makes an ideal serving dish for this carefully assembled Niçoise salad: Greens form a leafy bed for the tomatoes, green beans, bell pepper strips, potatoes, and chunks of tuna steak garnished with anchovies, capers, and Niçoise olives. French bread, lightly toasted with feta cheese on top, is served in a rustic basket.

Fresh Tuna Niçoise
French Bread with Feta Cheese and Olive Oil

Although canned tuna is a popular salad ingredient, few cooks think of using succulent fresh tuna steaks. Sold at many fish markets, fresh tuna looks like raw beef. It should not smell sour and should have moist elastic flesh. Refrigerate tuna steaks loosely wrapped in plastic, and use them as soon as possible. When they cook, they become firm and develop a strong but not unpleasant flavour. For the best results, allow the tuna to cool for at least 20 minutes after cooking, and serve it at room temperature in the salad. If fresh tuna is unnavailable, use canned water-packed tuna.

A mainstay of Greek cuisine, feta cheese is soft and crumbly, with a characteristic sharp, astringent taste. It is sold at delicatessen counters in most supermarkets and will stay fresh in the refrigerator for months if stored in salty water. Rinse it under cold water before using.

What to drink
A full-bodied white wine or a dry rosé, well chilled, is the best choice for this Provençal meal. Try a California Chardonnay or French Mâcon. For the rosé, purchase one from the south of France if possible. Tavel is excellent.

Start-to-Finish Steps
1 Follow tuna Niçoise recipe steps 1 to 24.
2 Follow French bread recipe steps 1 to 5 and serve with salad.

Fresh Tuna Niçoise

Three 2–2.5 cm (³/₄–1 inch) thick fresh tuna steaks
  (about 750 g (1¹/₂ lb) total weight)
1 lemon
Salt and freshly ground black pepper
250 ml (8 fl oz) plus 1 tablespoon olive oil
350 g (12 oz) small red or white potatoes
3 medium-size cloves garlic
60 g (2 oz) Niçoise or oil-cured black olives
1 bay leaf
250 g (8 oz) green beans
1 head lettuce, 1 bunch watercress, 500 g
  (1 lb) spinach, or combination of these greens

60 g (2 oz) jar capers
100 ml (3 fl oz) red wine vinegar
Small bunch fresh basil
350 g (12 oz) ripe tomatoes
Small green bell pepper
Small bunch scallions
60 g (2 oz) tin anchovy fillets, preferably salt-packed

1 Preheat oven to 190°C (450°F or Mark 8).
2 Place tuna steaks in non-aluminium baking dish in a single layer. Halve lemon crosswise and squeeze juice of one half over steaks; reserve remaining half for another use. sprinkle steaks lightly with salt and pepper and drizzle with 3 tablespoons olive oil. Turn steaks to coat both sides and set aside to marinate at least 15 minutes.
3 Wash potatoes under cold running water. Cut unpeeled potatoes crosswise into 1 cm (¹/₂ inch) thick rounds and place in medium-size saucepan. Add enough cold water to cover potatoes by 7.5 cm (3 inches) and bring to a boil over high heat.
4 Fill another medium-size saucepan two-thirds full with cold water, cover, and bring to a boil over high heat.
5 Crush 1 clove garlic under blade of chef's knife; remove and discard peel. In small bowl, combine olives, crushed garlic, bay leaf, and 2 tablespoons olive oil; toss to combine. Set aside to marinate.
6 Wash green beans under cold running water. Trim ends and discard. Cut beans lengthwise into halves or thirds, depending on size.
7 Reduce heat under potatoes to medium and cook 10 to 15 minutes, or until they can be pierced easily with tip of knife.
8 Add green beans to boiling water and cook 3 to 5 minutes, or until crisp-tender.
9 While beans are cooking, place tuna steaks on middle rack of oven and bake 8 minutes, or until opaque on outside and still pink in centre.
10 Turn beans into strainer and refresh under cold running water; set aside to cool.
11 Wash greens and dry in salad spinner or with paper towels. Tear into bite-size pieces, wrap in paper towels, and refrigerate until ready to assemble salad.
12 Remove tuna from oven and set aside to cool. Raise oven temperature to 230°C (450°F or Mark 8).
13 Turn potatoes into colander and refresh under cold running water; set aside to cool.

14 For dressing, crush remaining 2 cloves garlic under blade of chef's knife; discard peel. Drain 1 tablespoon capers and rinse under cold running water; chop coarsely. Combine garlic, capers, and red wine vinegar in small bowl. Whisking continuously, add remaining olive oil in a slow, steady stream and whisk until blended. Add $^1/_4$ teaspoon salt, and freshly ground black pepper to taste, and whisk until blended; set aside.

15 Wash and dry basil. Cut leaves crosswise into thin shreds to measure about 45 g (1$^1/_2$ oz); set aside.

16 Wash tomatoes and dry with paper towels. Core and quarter tomatoes. Halve each quarter crosswise.

17 Wash and dry green pepper. Core, halve, and seed pepper. Cut each half crosswise, then slice each quarter into thin strips; set aside.

18 Wash and dry scallions. Thinly slice scallions to measure about 100 g (3 oz); set aside.

19 Combine potatoes, green pepper, scallions, and half of basil in large bowl. Add a few tablespoons of dressing and toss to combine.

20 Combine tomatoes and remaining basil in medium-size bowl. Add a tablespoon of dressing and toss to combine.

21 Dry green beans with paper towels and place in another medium-size bowl. Add a tablespoon of dressing and toss to combine.

22 If using salt-packed anchovies, rinse thoroughly under cold running water, gently rubbing off salt with your fingers. Halve lengthwise and pull out bone. Rinse again and pat dry. If using oil-packed anchovies, rinse gently and pat dry with paper towels. Set anchovies aside.

23 Remove skin from tuna steaks and discard; break tuna into large chunks.

24 Line platter with salad greens. Spoon tuna into centre of platter and arrange potatoes, tomatoes, and green beans in mounds around tuna. Top tuna with anchovy fillets and dot platter with olives. Pour remaining dressing over salad and set aside until ready to serve.

French Bread with Feta Cheese and Olive Oil

1 baguette, or eight 2.5 cm (1 inch) thick slices
   regular French bread
125 g (4 oz) feta cheese
125 ml (8 fl oz) olive oil

1 Halve baguette crosswise and then lengthwise.
2 Arrange bread on baking sheet in a single layer.
3 Place half of feta cheese in small bowl, reserving remainder for another use. Crumble feta with fork. Add olive oil, and, using fork or whisk, blend with feta.
4 Spoon mixture over cut surfaces of baguette, or on one side of French bread slices, and toast in very hot oven about 4 minutes, or just until feta is golden.
5 Transfer hot bread to napkin-lined basket or bowl.

Smoked Ham and Fresh Spinach Salad with Creamy Mustard Mayonnaise
Deep-fried Onion Rings

Crisp fried onion rings complement ham, spinach, and potato salad with creamy mustard mayonnaise dressing.

When deep fried, the onion rings remain moist and tender under their crisp batter coating. For successful deep frying, slice the onions uniformly so that they cook at the same rate. Beat the eggs thoroughly, and be sure to coat the onions completely with egg and then the flour. If you do not have a deep-fat thermometer, you can test the oil by combining a spoonful of egg and flour to make a small ball of batter, then dropping it into the hot fat. If the batter sizzles on contact, the fat has reached the right frying temperature. Do not fry too many onion rings at one time; they should fit on the surface of the oil without crowding. Batter coat other vegetables, such as eggplant slices, broccoli, a cauliflower florets, or courgette cut lengthwise, to create an Italian-style deep-fry platter.

What to drink
These dishes would go well with a light, fruity red wine. The cook suggests Beaujolais. Other options are a young California Zinfandel, a Gamay Beaujolais, or an Italian Chianti or Dolcetto.

Start-to-Finish Steps
1 Follow ham and spinach recipe step 1 and onion ring recipe step 1.
2 Follow ham and spinach recipe steps 2 to 8.

3 Follow onion rings recipe steps 2 to 8.
4 Follow ham and spinach recipe step 9, onion rings recipe step 9, and serve.

Smoked Ham and Fresh Spinach Salad with Creamy Mustard Mayonnaise

350 g (12 oz) small red potatoes
2 large bunches spinach (750 g–1 Kg (1¹/₂–2 lb) total weight)
Small bunch fresh parsley
Small bunch fresh tarragon, or 4 teaspoon dried
Small bunch fresh chives or scallions
175 g (6 oz) mayonnaise
4 teaspoons Dijon mustard
2 tablespoons heavy cream
350 g (12 oz) mild smoked ham sliced very thinly
Freshly ground black pepper

1 Wash potatoes and slice into 5 mm (¹/₄ inch) thick rounds. Place in medium-size saucepan with enough cold water to cover potatoes by 7.5 cm (3 inches) and bring to a boil over high heat.
2 When water comes to a boil, reduce heat to medium and cook, uncovered, 10 to 15 minutes, or until potatoes can be pierced easily with tip of sharp knife.
3 While potatoes are boiling, remove and dicard stems from smaller spinach leaves, reserving large leaves for another use. Wash spinach thoroughly in several changes of cold water and dry in salad spinner or with paper towels. Line 4 plates with spinach leaves and set aside.
4 Transfer potatoes to colander and set aside to cool.
5 Wash parsley, and fresh tarragon if using, and dry with paper towels. Trim and discard stems from parsley and chop enough to measure 2 tablespoons; set aside. Reserve 4 sprigs tarragon to measure 1 teaspoon; set aside. reserve remaining herbs for another use.
6 Wash chives or scallions and dry with paper towels. Chop enough chives to measure 1 tablespoon. If using scallions, trim ends and discard. Chop enough green tops to measure 1 tablespoon; reserve remaining scallions for another use.
7 In small bowl, combine mayonnaise, mustard, cream, tarragon, and chives or scallions, and stir with fork until blended; set aside.
8 To assemble salad, loosely roll each slice of ham into cone shape and arrange slices in centre of each spinach-lined plate. Arrange potatoes on either side of ham and sprinkle with freshly ground black pepper to taste.
9 Drizzle each salad with 2 tablespoons creamy mustard mayonnaise, sprinkle with parsley, and serve remaining dressing on the side.

Deep-Fried Onion Rings

2 large yellow onions (about 750 g (1¹/₂ lb) total weight)
4 eggs
1¹/₂ ltrs (2¹/₂ pts) peanut oil
250 g (8 oz) plain flour
Salt

1 Peel and cut onions crosswise into 5 mm (¹/₄ inch) thick rounds. Separate into rings, discarding green centres; set aside.
2 Preheat oven to SLOW.
3 Break eggs into large bowl. Add 4 tablespoons water and beat with fork or whisk until well blended.
4 Add onion rings to egg mixture and stir with fork until well coated.
5 Pour peanut oil into large, deep heavy-gauge skillet and place skillet over medium-high heat.
6 Place flour in shallow baking dish.
7 Line a heatproof platter with paper towels.
8 When oil registers 190°C (375°F) on deep-fat thermometer, dredge onion rings, a handful at a time, in flour. Using tongs or mesh strainer, carefully lower rings into hot oil and deep fry, adjusting heat as necessary to keep temperature constant, about 3 minutes, or until golden. With mesh strainer, transfer onion rings to paper-towel-lined platter and keep warm in oven until ready to serve.
9 Just before serving, sprinkle onion rings lightly with salt and divide among 4 salad plates.

Shrimp and Pasta with Spinach Pesto
Italian Bread with Garlic, Thyme, and Olive Oil

Pesto, which originated in the city of Genoa, is a zesty uncooked herb sauce traditionally containing fresh basil, garlic, olive oil, Parmesan or Romano cheese, and pine nuts. It can be used as a pasta topping, a sauce for grilled meats or freshly sliced tomatoes, or as a garnish for soups and salads. The cook provides an unexpected twist to the standard pesto recipe by adding spinach, which intensifies the flavour of the fresh basil. When basil is out of season, substitute an equal amount of fresh parsley plus 1 teaspoon dried oregano or tarragon.

What to drink
The cook recommends a light Chianti with this menu, but you could also try a crisp acidic white wine such as Verdicchio or Pinot Grigio.

Start-to-Finish Steps
1 For shrimp and pasta recipe, peel 4 cloves garlic and put through garlic press held over small bowl. Repeat for remaining 4 cloves garlic and place in another small bowl for bread recipe. If using fresh thyme, rinse and dry with paper towels. Reserve 6 sprigs for shrimp and pasta recipe and strip enough leaves from remainder to measure 2 level tablespoons for bread recipe.
2 Follow shrimp and pasta recipe steps 1 to 13 and bread recipe step 1.
3 Follow shrimp and recipe steps 14 to 18.
4 Follow bread recipe steps 2 to 4.
5 While bread is toasting, follow shrimp and pasta recipe step 19.
6 Follow bread recipe step 5 and serve with shrimp and pasta.

Cooked shrimp form a decorative pinwheel on top of the salad of corkscrew pasta and fresh peas tossed with spinach pesto. Crusty bread coated with garlic, thyme, and olive oil is a fitting partner for the salad.

Shrimp and Pasta with Spinach Pesto

Medium-size yellow onion
2 peppercorns
6 sprigs fresh thyme, or $1/2$ teaspoon dried
2 bay leaves
250 ml (8 fl oz) tarragon vinegar
500 ml (1 pt) dry white wine
750 g ($1^1/2$ lb) fresh peas, or 300 g (10 oz) package frozen
500–750 g (1–$1^1/2$ lb) medium-size shrimp (about 28 shrimp)
350 g (12 oz) dry fusilli, shells, or linguine
1 bunch fresh spinach (about 500 g (1 lb))
Small bunch fresh basil
125 g (4 oz) Parmesan cheese
4 cloves garlic, peeled and pressed
250 ml (8 fl oz) olive oil
Salt
Freshly ground black pepper

1 Peel and halve onion. Coarsely chop one half; reserve remaining half for another use.
2 Crack peppercorns under flat blade of chef's knife.
3 Combine onion, cracked peppercorns, thyme, bay leaves, vinegar, white wine, and 2 ltrs ($3^1/2$ pts) cold water in large non-aluminium saucepan and bring to a boil, partially covered, over high heat.
4 Meanwhile, fill stockpot two-thirds full with cold water and bring to a boil over high heat.
5 Shell fresh peas, if using.
6 Pinch off legs of shrimp, several at a time, then bend back and snap off sharp, beaklike piece of shell just above tail. Remove shell and discard. Using sharp paring knife, make shallow incision along back of each shrimp, exposing black digestive vein. Extract black vein and discard. Rinse shrimp under cold running water, drain, and dry with paper towels. Set aside.
7 Reduce heat under poaching liquid in saucepan to medium-high and simmer 15 minutes.
8 Add peas to stockpot and cook 1 to 2 minutes, or until most peas rise to top. Remove peas immediately with large mesh strainer, reserving water in pot, and refresh under cold running water. Transfer peas to small bowl.
9 Return water in stockpot to a boil, add pasta, and cook according to package directions, until just past *al dente*.
10 While pasta is cooking, wash spinach in several changes of cold water; do not dry. Remove and discard tough stems. Cut leaves crosswise into 1 cm ($1/2$ inch) wide strips and place them in medium-size skillet.
11 Transfer pasta to colander and set aside to cool.
12 Add shrimp to poaching liquid and cook 5 minutes.
13 Place skillet over medium heat and cook spinach, stirring, 2 minutes, or until spinach is completely wilted. Transfer spinach to large sieve and set aside to cool.
14 Remove shrimp from from stockpot with mesh strainer and refresh under cold running water; set aside to cool 15 minutes. Reserve poaching liquid for another use. (If not using within 2 days, freeze in container with lid.)
15 Wash basil and dry with paper towels. Trim off stems and discard. Cut leaves crosswise into 1 cm ($1/2$ inch) wide strips and set aside.
16 Using food processor or grater, grate Parmesan.
17 When spinach is cool enough to handle, press with back of spoon to remove excess moisture. Transfer to food processor or blender.
18 Add garlic, basil, grated Parmesan, and olive oil to spinach and purée.
19 To assemble salad, combine pasta and peas in large bowl. Add salt and pepper to taste, and toss to combine. Add half the spinach pesto and toss until pasta is evenly coated. Divide among 4 bowls and top with shrimp. Serve with remaining spinach pesto on the side.

Italian Bread with Garlic, Thyme, and Olive Oil

1 long loaf Italian bread
4 cloves garlic, peeled and pressed
2 level tablespoons fresh thyme leaves, or 2 teaspoons dried
125 ml (4 fl oz) olive oil

1 Preheat oven to 230°C (450°F or Mark 8).
2 Halve bread lengthwise and place on baking sheet, cut sides up.
3 In small bowl, combine garlic, thyme, and olive oil, and stir with fork to combine. Using pastry brush, coat cut sides of bread with oil mixture.
4 Toast bread about 12 minutes, or just until golden.
5 Cut bread on diagonal into 7.5 cm (3 inch) wide slices and serve.

Connie Handa Moore

Menu 1
(*Right*)
Peasant-style Miso soup
Ham, Vegetable, and Noodle Salad
Strawberries with Frosted Sponge Fingers

The art of Japanese cooking involves treating all foods with respect – never overlooking them and paying careful attention to the way dishes are presented. 'Because we Japanese eat with our eyes,' says Connie Handa Moore, 'we want our meals to be aesthetically pleasing.' Her three Oriental-style salad menus are in keeping with this time-honoured tradition.

Menu 1 is a three-course meal that starts with a soup brimming with diced vegetables, tofu, and scallions, and flavoured with *miso*. The soup whets the palate for the salad of vegetables, ham, and noodles on crisp spinach leaves. Fresh whole strawberries and sponge fingers frosted with whipped cream and nuts are the tempting dessert.

The beautiful salad of Menu 2 makes a good luncheon or a light dinner. Large shrimp and ribbons of egg crêpe are arranged on a mixture of rice, peas, and *shiitake* mushrooms. The colourful shrimp complement the orange mousse dessert, which can be placed on the table with the main course for visual appeal.

Presentation is again the key in Menu 3. Here strips of beef and mushrooms are stir-fried briefly, then placed on a contrasting bed of crisp shredded cabbage coated with a light vinaigrette. Tomato pudding, topped with rings of green bell pepper, is the bright side dish.

The miso soup garnished with scallions is served in lidded bowls to retain heat. It precedes the ham, vegetable, and noodle salad with strips of cucumber and courgette, and the light dessert of fresh strawberries with frosted sponge fingers.

**Peasant-style Miso Soup
Ham, Vegetable, and Noodle Salad
Strawberries with Frosted Sponge Fingers**

Bamboo shoots are a main ingredient in the soup. Most often associated with Chinese cookery, these tender young shoots of tropical bamboo plants have a slightly sweet taste and a crisp texture. They are sold whole or sliced in cans and have the best flavour when packed in water rather than brine.

What to drink

Enjoy a firm, dry white wine with this menu. Sancerre and Pouilly-Fumé would both be excellent, as would their California cousin Sauvignon Blanc.

Start-to-Finish Steps
1 Follow strawberries recipe steps 1 to 5.
2 Follow salad recipe steps 1 to 12.
3 Follow soup recipe steps 1 to 8 and strawberries recipe step 6.
4 Follow soup recipe step 9 and serve as first course.
5 Follow salad recipe step 13 and serve.
6 Follow strawberries recipe step 7 and serve.

Peasant-style Miso Soup

1 ltr (1³/₄ pts) chicken stock, preferably homemade
Large carrot, or small daikon radish (about 125 g (4 oz))
250 g (8 oz) can bamboo shoots
5 level tablespoons white miso paste
175 g (6 oz) firm tofu
1 scallion

1 Place chicken stock in medium-size saucepan. Cover and bring to a boil over medium heat.
2 While stock is heating, peel and trim carrot or daikon. Cut into small dice.
3 Turn bamboo shoots into colander, rinse under cold running water, and drain,. Coarsely chop enough bamboo shoots to measure 125 g (4 oz).
4 Add vegetables to stock and return to a boil. Reduce heat, cover, and gently simmer vegetables about 5 minutes, or until crisp-tender.
5 While soup is simmering, measure miso into small

bowl. Add 1 tablespoon hot tap water and stir until thoroughly blended. Set aside.
6 Rinse tofu under cold running water; pat dry with paper towel. Cut tofu into small dice; set aside.
7 Rinse scallion and dry with paper towel. Trim ends and discard. Cut on diagonal into 5 mm (¹/₄ inch) slices; set aside.
8 Turn miso into soup and stir until blended. Raise heat to medium-high and bring soup to a boil.
9 As soon as soup comes to a boil, remove pan from heat. Add tofu to soup and divide among individual bowls. Sprinkle with sliced scallion and serve.

Ham, Vegetable, and Noodle salad

Small bunch large-leaf spinach (about 250 g (8 oz))
Large red onion
350 g (12 oz) cherry tomatoes
Medium-size cucumber
Medium-size courgette
625 g (1¹/₄ lb) ham
125 ml (4 fl oz) plus 1 tablespoon vegetable oil
500 g (1 lb) fresh Chinese egg noodles, or 350 g (12 oz) dried capellini or spaghettini
Medium-size lemon
175 g (6 oz) granulated sugar
Salt and freshly ground pepper
125 ml (4 fl oz) white vinegar

1 In large saucepan or stockpot, bring 4¹/₂ ltrs (8 pts) of water to a rapid boil.
2 Meanwhile, remove and discard any bruised or discoloured spinach leaves. Wash remaining leaves in several changes of cold water; remove tough stems. Shake leaves and drain in colander; set aside.
3 Peel and halve red onion. Cut into thin slices. Cut slices in half and separate into strips; set aside.
4 Wash and dry cherry tomatoes. Remove stems.
5 Wash and dry cucumber. Trim ends and discard. Halve cucumber crosswise and then halve each piece lengthwise. Cut quarters lengthwise into julienne.
6 Under cold running water, scrub courgette with vegetable brush to remove sand; dry with paper

46

towel. Cut courgette into julienne; set aside.

7   Cut ham into julienne; set aside.

8   Add 1 tablespoon oil to boiling water to prevent noodles from sticking together. Add noodles, stir with wooden spoon to separate, and cook 2 to 3 minutes for fresh, or according to package directions for dried.

9   Squeeze lemon to measure 2 tablespoons juice.

10 Turn noodles into colander and rinse under cold running water; set aside to drain.

11 For dressing, combine sugar, 2 teaspoons salt, $1/2$ teaspoon pepper, vinegar, lemon juice, and 125 ml (4 fl oz) oil in small bowl and beat with fork until blended; set aside.

12 Divide spinach among 4 dinner plates. Divide noodles among plates, mounding them in centre. Top noodles with cucumber, courgette, and onion. Arrange cherry tomatoes and ham strips decoratively around noodles; cover and set aside until ready to serve.

13 Just before serving, stir dressing to recombine and serve with salads.

Strawberries with Frosted Sponge Fingers

500–750 g (1–1$1/2$ lb) strawberries, preferably with
  stems, or raspberries
100 g (3 oz) walnut pieces
250 ml (8 fl oz) heavy cream
4 to 8 sponge fingers
30 g (1 oz) confectioners' sugar

1   Place medium-size bowl and beaters for whipping cream in freezer to chill.

2   Leave stems on strawberries and gently rinse berries under cold running water. Transfer to a double thickness of paper towels and pat dry. Divide berries among 4 dessert plates; set aside.

3   Coarsely chop walnuts set aside.

4   Pour cream into chilled bowl. Using electric mixer, whip cream until soft peaks form.

5   Separate sponge fingers into single sections and spread each half with a layer of whipped cream. Sprinkle with walnuts and divide sponge fingers among plates with berries. Cover each serving with plastic wrap and refrigerate.

6   Twenty minutes before serving, remove plates from refrigerator.

7   When ready to serve, place confectioners' sugar in small bowl and serve separately with strawberries and sponge fingers.

Added Touch

For an impressive appetizer or *hors d'oeuvre*, sculpture cucumber sections into attractive cups to hold slices of smoked salmon.

Cucumber Cups with Gravlax and Capers

1 head lettuce
Small lemon
1 large cucumber (about 40 cm (16 inches) long)
12 thin slices gravlax or Nova lox
4 teaspoons capers, rinsed and drained

1   Wash and dry lettuce. Remove any bruised or discoloured leaves. Divide among 4 salad plates; set aside.

2   Wash and dry lemon. Cut crosswise into four 5 mm ($1/4$ inch) thick slices; set aside.

3   Wash and dry cucumber. Trim ends and discard. With sharp paring knife, cut cucumber croswise into approximately 10 cm (4 inch) quarters. Cut 2.5 cm (1 inch) deep triangles around one end of each quaerter to form crown shape. Using melon baller or teaspoon, scoop out inside, leaving 5 mm ($1/4$ inch) of flesh at bottom, to form cup for filling.

4   Stuff each cucumber cup with two slices of gravlax and top with 1 teaspoon capers.

5   Divide cucumber cups among lettuce-lined plates. Fold remaining slices of gravlax into cone shape and place one next to each cucumber cup. Garnish each plate with a lemon slice and serve.

<table>
<tr><td>

Menu

2

</td><td>

Shrimp and Vegetable Rice
Japanese Orange Mousse

</td></tr>
</table>

Golden ribbons of egg garnish this beautifully composed salad of shrimp, vegetables, and rice. The dessert is orange mousse.

Thin, delicate ribbons of egg make an unusual topping for the shrimp and vegetable rice salad. Before cooking, lightly grease skillet with oil, heat the skillet, then slowly pour in just enough beaten egg mixture to form a paper-thin sheet. As you pour, rotate the hot skillet so the egg is evenly distibuted. Do not allow the egg to brown; the finished egg strips should be pale yellow. Slice the cooked egg thinly –the thinner slices, the more delicate they appear. You can vary the salad by substituting drained canned tuna or poached chicken slices for the cooked shrimp.

The foamy orange mousse is garnished with Mandarin orange, whipped cream, mint leaves, and slivers of crystallized ginger. Mandarin oranges originated in China and are similar to tangerines, which can be substituted. Crystallized, or candied, ginger is covered with sugar, so use it sparingly or the dessert will be too sweet.

What to drink
The cook recommends a fruity white wine with a touch of sweetness: Vouvray is the first choice, or try California Chenin blanc or German Riesling.

Start-to-Finish Steps
One hour ahead: Set out frozen peas to thaw at room temperature.

Thirty minutes ahead: Remove vanilla ice cream from freezer and set out until it has a semi-soft but still firm consistency.

1   Follow mousse recipe steps 1 to 8.
2   Follow rice recipe steps 1 to 20 and serve with mousse.

Pinch off legs to remove shell.

Shrimp and Vegetable Rice

350 g (12 oz) long-grain rice
3 teaspoons salt
625 g (1¼ lb) large shrimp
8 dried shiitake mushrooms (about 125 g (4 oz) total weight), or 250 g (8 oz) fresh button mushrooms
125 g (4 oz) plus ½ teaspoon sugar
Medium-size carrot
125 g (8 oz) can whole water chestnuts
300 g (10 oz) package frozen peas, thawed
1 egg
30 g (1 oz) walnuts or almonds
5 tablespoons white vinegar
1 teaspoon dry white wine
100 g (3 oz) mayonnaise
2 teaspoons Japanese soy sauce
1 level tablespoon ketchup
Hot pepper sauce

1   In medium-size heavy-gauge saucepan, bring 750 ml (1½ pts) of water to a rapid boil over high heat. Add rice and 1 teaspoon salt, return to a boil, and stir rice with wooden spoon. Cover pan, reduce heat, and simmer 20 minutes.
2   While rice simmers, bring 4½ ltrs (8 pts) of water to a rapid boil in stockpot over high heat.
3   While water is heating, peel and devein shrimp (see following illustration): Pinch off legs of shrimp, several at a time, then bend back and snap off sharp, beaklike pieces of shell just above tail. Remove shell and discard. Using sharp paring knife, make shallow incision along back of each shrimp, exposing black digestive vein. Extract black vein with your fingers and discard. Place shrimp in colander; rinse under cold running water, and drain.
4   Add shrimp to boiling water in stockpot and cook 3 to 4 minutes, or until backs of shrimp turn opaque and begin to curl.
5   Fluff rice with fork and turn into large bowl; set aside to cool. Rinse saucepan.
6   Turn shrimp into colander and refresh under cold running water; set aside to cool.

Extract digestive vein with your fingers.

7   Bring 750 ml (1¹/₂ pts) of water to a boil in medium-size saucepan over high heat. If using button mushrooms, wipe clean with damp paper towels; leave whole. Add 60 g (2 oz) sugar, 1 teaspoon salt, and shiitake or button mushrooms to boiling water and stir. When water returns to a boil, cover pan, reduce heat, and simmer 15 minutes for shiitake or 5 minutes for button mushrooms.

8   While mushrooms are simmering, bring 250 ml (8 fl oz) of water to a boil in small saucepan over medium-high heat.

9   Meanwhile, peel and trim carrot. Halve crosswise and then halve each piece lengthwise. Cut quarters into 2.5 cm (1 inch) long slivers.

10 Add carrot to boiling water and blanch 1 minute. Turn into large strainer and refresh under cold running water. Transfer to small plate and set aside to cool.

11 Turn water chestnuts into strainer and rinse under cold running water; dry with paper towels. Cut into very thin slices; set aside.

12 Turn thawed peas into strainer and drain. Transfer to small bowl and set aside.

13 Turn mushrooms into strainer and rinse under cold running water; drain. Transfer mushrooms to double thickness of paper towels and press to remove excess moisture. Remove and discard stems of shiitake and cut caps into very thin slices; if using button mushrooms, leave whole. Set mushrooms aside.

14 Using paper towel that has been dipped in oil, grease large nonstick skillet and heat over medium-high heat until hot.

15 Meanwhile, crack egg into small bowl. Add ¹/₂ teaspoon sugar and 1 teaspoon water, and whisk until blended. Slowly pour just enough egg into pan barely to coat bottom and cook about 1 minute or until crêpe appears dry; do *not* allow to brown. When set, loosen edge of crêpe with rubber spatula

and flip over onto clean work surface. Regrease pan, beat egg to recombine, and repeat until all egg mixture is used.

16 Stack crêpes and roll stack into cylinder. Using a sharp knife, cut crosswise into very thin strips. Transfer strips to a plate and toss to separate; set aside.

17 Coarsely chop walnuts; set aside.

18 For vinaigrette, combine white vinegar, 60 g (2 oz) sugar, 1 teaspoon salt, and white wine in small bowl and whisk until blended.

19 Combine mayonnaise, soy sauce, ketchup, and dash of hot pepper sauce in a small bowl and stir until blended. Turn into serving dish and set aside.

20 Add mushrooms, carrots, water chestnuts, and vinaigrette to rice and stir with wooden spoon to combine. Divide mixture among 4 dinner plates and sprinkle with drained peas. Top with equal portions of egg strips and arrange shrimp around border of each plate. Sprinkle with nuts and serve with spicy mayonnaise on the side.

Japanese Orange Mousse

Small bunch mint
45 g (1¹/₂ oz) crystallized ginger
300 g (10 oz) can Mandarin oranges
Two 100 g (3 oz) packages orange-flavoured gelatin
2 tablespoons orange-flavoured liqueur
500 ml (1 pt) vanilla ice cream, semi-soft
125 ml (4 fl oz) heavy cream

1   Place medium-size bowl and beaters for whipping cream in freezer to chill.

2   Rinse mint and dry with paper towels. Set aside 12 leaves for garnish; refrigerate remainder for another use.

3   Slice ginger into thin slivers; set aside.

4   Drain Mandarin oranges; set aside.

5   In small saucepan, bring 250 ml (8 fl oz) of water to a boil over high heat. Add orange-flavoured gelatin and stir with wooden spoon until thoroughly dissolved.

6   Pour gelatin mixture into large bowl, add 3 ice cubes and liqueur, and stir until ice melts. Add ice cream and whisk by hand until light and fluffy. Cover mixture with plastic wrap and place in freezer.

7   Pour heavy cream into chilled bowl and beat with electric mixer until cream stands in soft peaks.

8   Divide mousse among 4 serving bowls or goblets and top each serving with a spoonful of whipped cream. Arrange orange slices and mint leaves decoratively around whipped cream. Garnish whipped cream with ginger slices. Cover desserts with plastic wrap and refrigerate until ready to serve.

Glazed Beef and Mushrooms with Shredded Cabbage
Baked Tomato Pudding

For a quick family meal, serve beef and mushrooms on a bed of shredded cabbage coated with vinaigrette dressing. Baked tomato pudding garnished with green pepper rings is the vegetable side dish.

The stir-fried beef strips are glazed with a sauce seasoned with *mirin*, a sweet rice wine that is frequently used in Japanese cooking. Once opened, *mirin* lasts for several months on a pantry shelf and indefinitely in the refrigerator. If you cannot locate it in a speciality food store, you can make your own by combining equal parts sherry and sugar, then cooking the mixture over low heat until syrupy.

What to drink
The spiciness of a well-chilled California Gewürztraminer would enhance the varied flavours of this meal. An Alsatian or Italian Gewürztraminer is also good.

Start-to-Finish Steps
1 Follow tomato pudding recipe steps 1 to 9.
2 While tomato pudding is baking, follow salad recipe steps 1 to 15.
3 Follow tomato pudding recipe step 10 and salad recipe steps 16 to 18.
4 Follow tomato pudding recipe steps 11 and 12, and serve with salad.

Glazed Beef and Mushrooms with Shredded Cabbage

2 level tablespoons sesame seeds
175 g (6 oz) sugar
125 ml (4 fl oz) plus 1 tablespoon vegetable oil
4 tablespoons white vinegar
1 teaspoon salt
$1/2$ teaspoon freshly ground black pepper
Small bunch fresh coriander for garnish (optional)
Small head Chinese or Savoy cabbage (about 500 g (1 lb))
8 medium-size mushrooms (about 175 g (6 oz) total weight)
2 scallions
5 cm (2 inch) piece fresh ginger
Large clove garlic
1 level tablespoon cornstarch
4 tablespoons Japanese soy sauce
2 tablespoons mirin
625–750 g ($1^1/4$ – $1^1/2$ lb) boneless sirloin or other lean beef, cut into 5 cm (2 inch) wide strips
500 g (1 lb) can large pitted black olives

51

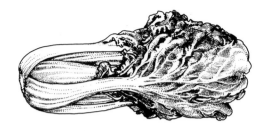

Chinese cabbage   *Fresh ginger*

1 In small heavy-gauge skillet, roast sesame seeds over medium heat, shaking skillet to prevent scorching. When seeds start to pop, remove skillet from heat. Set aside.
2 For vinaigrette, combine 3 level tablespoons sugar, 125 ml (4 fl oz) vinegar, salt, and pepper in small bowl and beat with fork until blended; set aside.
3 Wash coriander, if using, and dry with paper towels. Trim off root ends, leaving 5 cm (2 inch) long sprigs. Wrap in paper towels and refrigerate until ready to serve.
4 Wash cabbage and dry with paper towels. Quarter cabbage; remove and discard core. Using food processor fitted with slicing disc, feed each quarter into tube, with core side at right angle to disc, and pulse until all cabbage is sliced. Or, thinly slice each quarter with chef's knife.
5 Place cabbage in large bowl and add enough iced water to cover; set aside.
6 Wipe mushrooms clean with damp paper towels.

Remove and discard stems. Cut caps into very thin slices; set aside.
7 Wash scallions and dry with paper towels. Trim ends and discard. Thinly slice scallions; set aside.
8 Grate enough ginger to measure 2 teaspoons; set aside.
9 Peel and mince garlic; set aside.
10 Combine cornstarch, soy sauce, remaining sugar, mirin, and ginger in small bowl and stir to combine. Pour into medium-size skillet and heat over medium heat, stirring constantly with a wooden spoon, 1 to 2 minutes, or until sauce thickens and starts to bubble. Remove skillet from heat and set aside.
11 Transfer cabbage to colander and shake to drain as much water as possible. Dry large bowl. Return cabbage to bowl, cover with plastic wrap, and refrigerate.
12 Heat 1 tablespoon oil in large heavy-gauge skillet over high heat for 30 seconds. Reduce heat to medium-low, add garlic and scallions, and stir 1 minute. With slotted spoon, transfer garlic and scallions to measuring cup; set aside.
13 Using same skillet, quickly stir-fry meat over medium-high heat about 3 minutes, or until it loses its pink colour.
14 Add mushrooms to meat and cook another 30 seconds. Transfer meat and mushrooms to colander and drain.
15 Return meat and mushrooms to skillet, add sautéed scallions and garlic and sauce, and stir to combine. Remove pan from heat and set aside.
16 Drain olives; set aside.
17 Stir dressing to recombine. Remove cabbage from refrigerator, add dressing, and toss until evenly coated.
18 Divide cabbage among 4 dinner plates, making well in centre of cabbage. Spoon meat and mushroom mixture into wells. Sprinkle cabbage with toasted sesame seeds. Garnish each serving with large black olives and sprigs of coriander, if desired.

Baked Tomato Pudding

1 teaspoon vegetable oil
850 g (1³/₄ lb) can crushed tomatoes
Small onion
Large fresh basil leaf, or 1 tablespoon dried
5 level teaspoons unsalted butter
1 slice firm white bread
3 level tablespoons sugar
Salt and freshly ground white pepper
2 level tablespoons unseasoned bread crumbs
1 Italian green pepper for garnish

1 Preheat oven to 180°C (350°F or Mark 4). Set rack in top half of oven.
2 Grease four large ramekins or ovenproof dishes with vegetable oil.
3 Pour tomatoes into medium-size bowl.
4 Peel and finely chop enough onion to measure 45 g (1¹/₂ oz). Wash basil leaf, if using, and chop finely.
5 Melt 1 teaspoon butter in small heavy-gauge skillet over medium heat. Add onion and basil, and sauté, stirring occasionally, 3 to 5 minutes, or until onion is soft and translucent.
6 While onion is sautéing, cut bread slice into 1 cm (¹/₂ inch) cubes and add to tomatoes.
7 Add onion and basil mixture, sugar, salt, and a pinch of pepper to tomatoes; stir to combine. Rinse and dry skillet.
8 Divide tomato pudding mixture among prepared ramekins or dishes, smoothing tops with spatula. Sprinkle bread crumbs lightly over puddings and dot each serving with 1 teaspoon of remaining butter.
9 Reduce oven temperature to 170°C (325°F or Mark 3) and bake puddings in top half of oven 30 minutes.
10 Turn off heat and keep warm in oven until ready to serve.
11 Just before serving, wash pepper and dry with paper towel. Slice pepper into very thin rings; remove and discard ribs and seeds.
12 Remove puddings from oven, garnish with pepper rings, and serve.

Added Touch

Soba noodles, snow peas, and scallions flavoured with soy sauce and sesame oil make a substantial accompaniment for this salad.

Soba Noodles with Snow Peas and Scallions

125 g (4 oz) snow peas
3 scallions
300 g (10 oz) package soba noodles
3 tablespoons soy sauce
3 tablespoons sesame oil

1 Bring 3³/₄ ltrs (6 pts) of water to a boil in stockpot over high heat. Bring 500 ml (1 pt) of water to a boil in small saucepan over medium-high heat.
2 Rinse snow peas under cold running water. Remove and discard strings. Add peas to small saucepan of boiling water. When water returns to a boil, turn peas into strainer and refresh under cold running water; set aside.
3 Wash and dry scallions. Trim ends and discard. Cut scallions crosswise into 5 mm (¹/₄ inch) thick slices; set aside.
4 Add noodles to stockpot of boiling water and stir with wooden spoon to separate. Cover pot to help water return to a boil; then remove cover and continue cooking noodles 6 minutes, stirring occasionally.
5 Turn noodles into colander and rinse under hot running water for 30 seconds to remove starch.
6 Turn noodles into large mixing bowl, add soy sauce and sesame oil, and toss until evenly coated.
7 Divide noodles among 4 plates, sprinkle with scallions and snow peas, and serve.

Susan Huberman

Menu 1
(*left*)
Crudités with Cavier Dip
Crabmeat and Mushroom Salad

As a professional food stylist, Susan Huberman must make every dish she prepares look appealing, so she is particularly conscious of how the colours, shapes, and textures of foods work together. Naturally, when cooking at home, she is aware of the same things, but she is also wary of preparing fastidiously arranged dishes that might imtimidate her guests. 'I want people to dig in and enjoy my food,' she says. 'No one should be afraid to eat a meal because it appears too elaborate.' The three salad menus offered here are not only inviting but also taste as good as they look.

Menus 1 and 3 are for occasions when you want to impress special friends. The cook describes Menu 1 as a sensual dinner because it is especially pleasing to the palate. There is the luxury of caviar in the first course, folowed by fresh crabmeat and mushrooms. Menu 3 consists of three very different but elegant salads: warm duck with mango chutney, rice with pecans and mint, and sliced oranges and radishes spiced with cinnamon dressing.

Menu 2 is a colourful Italian meal, ideal for late summer when peppers and basil abound. Susan Huberman roasts the peppers and combines them with sun-dried tomatoes, mozzarella, basil leaves, and vinaigrette. With this she offers fresh pasta tossed with vegetables and Genoa salami, and a mixed green salad with pears.

A selection of fresh vegetables with a cavier dip makes an excellent cocktail-hour hors d'oeuvre or a perfect first course. Follow this with crabmeat and mushroom salad.

Crudités with Cavier Dip
Crabmeat and Mushroom Salad

Caviar is the roe of the sturgeon, but the generic term includes the roe of other fish as well, such as the lumpfish. Lumpfish caviar, used here in the dip, is not expensive and adds instant elegance to any menu.

What to drink
A dry white wine is called for here. For full body and fruitiness, choose a California Chardonnay; for crispness, an Italian Pinot Grigio or Pinot Bianco; for delicacy and charm, a Moselle Riesling.

Start-to-Finish Steps
1 Wash lettuce for both recipes and dry. Wrap in paper towels for salad recipe and refrigerate.
2 Follow crudités recipe steps 1 through 6.
3 Follow salad recipe steps 1 to 11.
4 Follow crudités recipe step 7 and serve as first course.
5 Follow salad recipe step 12 and serve.

Crudités with Caviar Dip

Small yellow or white onion
125 g (4 oz) whipped cream cheese
125 ml (4 fl oz) sour cream
60 g (2 oz) red lumpfish caviar
1 bunch scallions
1 bunch red radishes
1 bunch baby carrots
500 g (1 lb) whole white baby turnips
2 small yellow squash (about 250 g (8 oz) total weight)
Medium-sized red bell pepper
7 or 8 outer leaves lettuce

1 Halve and peel onion. Finely chop enough to measure 2 tablespoons; reserve remainder for another use.
2 Using processor, process cream cheese until smooth. Add sour cream and blend well. Add onion and process just until combined. Turn mixture into serving bowl.
3 If necessary, drain caviar; then gently fold into dip, reserving 1/2 teaspoon for garnish; cover and set aside.
4 Trim vegetables. Wash and dry with paper towels. Peel carrots and turnips. Cut squash on diagonal into 5 mm (1/4 inch) thick slices. Set vegetables aside.
5 Wash and dry red bell pepper. Halve, core, and seed pepper, cut lengthwise into 1 cm (1/2 inch) wide strips.
6 Line serving platter with lettuce leaves. Place bowl of dip on platter and arrange vegetables decoratively around it. Cover with plastic wrap and refrigerate until ready to serve.

7 Just before serving, sprinkle dip with reserved caviar.

Crabmeat and Mushroom Salad

500 g (1 lb) fresh or frozen crabmeat
125 g (4 oz) fresh shiitake, oyster, morel, or chanterelle mushrooms
4 to 6 shallots
100 ml (3 fl oz) olive oil, approximately
2 limes
Salt
Freshly ground pepper
Small bunch fresh coriander or parsley
175 g (6 oz) cherry tomatoes
2 heads lettuce
Red cabbage, watercress and lamb's lettuce for garnish

1 Place crabmeat in medium-size bowl. Remove any cartilage or bits of shell and discard. Flake crabmeat with fork; set aside.
2 Wipe mushrooms with damp paper towels. Cut off stem ends and discard. Cut mushrooms into 5 mm (1/4 inch) thick slices and set aside.
3 Peel and coarsely chop enough shallots to measure 3 tablespoons.
4 In small skillet or sauté pan, heat olive oil over medium heat. Add shallots and sauté, stirring occasionally, 3 minutes, or until soft.
5 Meanwhile, squeeze enough lime juice to measure 4 tablespoons; set aside.
6 Add mushrooms to skillet and sauté, stirring occasionally, another 10 minutes.
7 With slotted spoon, transfer mushrooms to bowl with crabmeat. Reserve oil in pan.
8 For dressing, add enough oil to reserved oil in skillet to measure 125 ml (4 fl oz). Add lime juice, season, and whisk until blended; set aside.
9 Wash coriander or parsley and dry with paper towels. Chop enough to measure 15 g (1/2 oz); add to crabmeat.
10 Wash and dry cherry tomatoes; remove and discard stems. Halve tomatoes; add to bowl with crabmeat.
11 Whisk dressing to recombine and pour over salad; toss until salad ingredients are evenly coated. Cover with plastic wrap and refrigerate until ready to serve.
12 Divide lettuce among 4 dinner plates and top with equal portions of salad.
13 Garnish with red cabbage, watercress and lamb's lettuce as illustrated.

Roasted Peppers with Mozzarella and Sun-Dried Tomatoes
Pasta and Vegetables with Genoa Salami
Pear, Watercress, and Belgian Endive Salad

For a particularly dazzling presentation, serve all three of these Italian salads on the same plate.

Mild mozzarella cheese is delicious with *pumate* (Italian sun-dried tomatoes with a highly concentrated flavour) and red, green, and yellow roasted peppers. *Pumate* are sold dried or oil packed at speciality food shops and Italian groceries. Although they are expensive, these tomatoes are well worth serving as a special treat. There are no substitutes.

Fresh *fusilli* (corkscrew pasta) tastes best in the salad, but you can use packaged dried *fusilli* if fresh is unavailable. This salad can be prepared the night before you plan to serve it, but be sure the pasta is cooked *al dente*, or it will get soggy in the dressing.

What to drink
A young Italian Chianti, Dolcetto, or Barbera would be good here. Or, if you prefer a domestic wine, consider a young Californian Gamay Beaujolais.

Start-to-Finish Steps
1 Peel and coarsely chop garlic for peppers recipe and pear salad recipe.
2 Follow pasta salad recipe steps 1 to 6.
3 While vegetables are steaming, follow peppers recipe steps 1 to 3.
4 While peppers are grilling, follow pasta salad recipe steps 7 to 11.
5 Follow peppers recipe step 4.
6 While peppers are steaming, follow pasta salad recipe steps 12 to 15.
7 Follow peppers recipe steps 5 to 9.
8 Follow pear salad recipe steps 1 to 7, pasta salad recipe step 16, peppers recipe step 10, and serve.

Roasted Peppers with Mozzarella and Sun-Dried Tomatoes

2 each red, green, and yellow bell peppers, or any combination
250 g (8 oz) fresh mozzarella cheese, or 250 g (8 oz) package good-quality mozzarella
1 bunch fresh basil, or 1 level tablespoon dried
4 tablespoons good-quality olive oil
2 tablespoons red wine vinegar
2 cloves garlic, coarsely chopped
125 g (4 oz) sun-dried tomatoes

1 Set grill pan 10 cm (4 inches) from heating element and preheat grill.
2 Wash and dry peppers. Halve, core, and seed.
3 Arrange peppers, skin-side up, on rack in grill pan. grill peppers 10 minutes, or until skins are blackened.
4 Using metal tongs, transfer peppers to brown paper bag, close bag, and set peppers aside to steam about 10 minutes.

57

5 Remove peppers from paper bag. Holding each half under cold running water, gently rub off blackened skin; dry with paper towels.

6 Cut cheese into 5 mm (¼ inch) thick slices.

7 Wash fresh basil, if using, and dry with paper towels. Strip leaves from stems; discard stems.

8 In small bowl, combine oil, vinegar, garlic, and dried basil if using, and beat with fork until blended.

9 Pour half the dressing into large shallow dish. Add peppers and cheese slices, overlapping and alternating slices of each. Top with fresh basil leaves if using, and tomatoes and drizzle with remaining dressing, if desired. Set aside until ready to serve.

10 Divide peppers and cheese among dinner plates.

Pasta and Vegetables with Genoa Salami

Medium-size courgette
Small bunch scallions
2 medium-size carrots (about 250 g (8 oz) total weight)
125 g (4 oz) frozen green peas
175 g (6 oz) can pitted black olives
4 tablespoons good-quality olive oil
2 tablespoons red wine vinegar
Salt and freshly ground pepper
125 g (4 oz) fresh or dried green fusilli
125 g (4 oz) fresh or dried white fusilli
175 g (6 oz) jar whole pimientos
60 g (2 oz) thinly sliced Genoa salami (about 6 slices)

1 Wash courgette and scallions, and dry with paper towels. Trim of ends and discard. Cut courgette crosswise into thin rounds; set aside. Thinly slice enough scallions to measure 30 g (1 oz); reserve remaining scallions for another use.

2 Peel and trim carrots. Cut crosswise into thin slices.

3 Fit medium-size saucepan with vegetable steamer and fill pan with enough water to come up to but not above bottom of steamer. Bring water to a boil over medium-high heat.

4 Place peas in small bowl of cold water to thaw.

5 Add carrots and courgettes to pan, cover, and steam about 5 minutes, or until courgette is just tender when pierced with the tip of a sharp knife and carrots are still crisp.

6 Meanwhile, in large saucepan, bring 3¾ ltrs (6 pts) of water to a boil over high heat.

7 Transfer steamed vegetables to large bowl.

8 Drain peas and add to vegetables.

9 Drain olives, halve lengthwise, and add to vegetables.

10 Combine olive oil, vinegar, and salt and pepper to taste in small bowl, and beat with fork until blended. Add to vegetables and toss until evenly coated.

11 Add 1 tablespoon salt and the pasta to boiling water, and cook, stirring frequently, 2 to 3 minutes for fresh pasta, 8 to 12 minutes for dried, or until *al dente*.

12 Turn pasta into colander to drain. Add warm pasta to vegetable mixture and toss gently to combine. Set aside to cool to room temperature, tossing mixture occasionally.

13 Rinse pimientos under cold running water and dry. Cut lengthwise into very thin strips.

14 Stack salami slices and cut into very thin strips.

15 When pasta has cooled, add pimientos and salami to bowl, and toss to combine. Adjust balance of oil and vinegar, and correct seasoning, if necessary. Cover salad with plastic wrap and refrigerate until ready to serve.

16 Just before serving, remove salad from refrigerator and toss to recombine. Divide salad among dinner plates.

Pear, Watercress, and Belgian Endive Salad

1 bunch watercress
2 heads Belgian endive
1 lemon
2 firm pears
1 egg
100 g (3 oz) Dijon mustard
175 ml (6 fl oz) red wine vinegar
2 cloves garlic, coarsely chopped
350 ml (12 fl oz) good-quality olive oil
Salt and freshly ground pepper

1 Wash watercress thoroughly and dry with paper towels. Break into bite-size pieces; set aside.

2 Rinse and dry endive. Trim off stem ends and discard. Cut endive crosswise into 1 cm (½ inch) wide pieces; set aside.

3 Halve lemon and squeeze 1 tablespoon juice into medium-size bowl. Reserving remaining half of lemon for another use. Add cold water to fill bowl two-thirds full.

4 Peel and halve pears lengthwise; core. Cut each half lengthwise into thin slices. Place pear slices in bowl with lemon water to prevent discolouration; set aside.

5 For dressing, combine egg, mustard, vinegar, and garlic in blender or food processor. With machine running, add olive oil in a slow, steady stream and process until dressing is thick and smooth. Add salt and pepper to taste and process dressing just until blended.

6 Drain pears and dry with paper towels.

7 Divide watercress and endive among 4 dinner plates and top with pear slices. Spoon some dressing over each salad and serve remaining dressing on the side, if desired.

Warm Duck Salad with Mango Chutney
Rice with Pecans and Mint
Orange and Radish Salad with Cinnamon

Dark tableware enhances the rich colours of duck with mango chutney, rice with pecans, and orange and radish salad.

Most supermarkets sell frozen whole ducks, but because duck is increasingly in demand, you can sometimes find fresh or frozen breasts, which are needed for the duck salad. Roasted duck skin, or crackling, is the garnish.

Water chestnuts, also an ingredient in the salad, are not nuts at all but tubers of an aquatic plant. Whole or sliced canned water chestnuts are sold in the Oriental food section of most supermarkets. Occasionally, fresh water chestnuts are available at Chinese groceries. If you use fresh, boil them whole for 15 minutes, cool slightly, then peel and use them as directed in the recipe.

What to drink
Serve a Gewürztraminer or a dry Alsatian Riesling with this menu. If you prefer a touch of sweetness, select a German Riesling from the Rhine area.

Start-to-Finish Steps
1 Wash fresh mint or parsley, and dry with paper towels. Reserve 4 mint sprigs for orange and radish salad recipe, and mince enough mint to measure 15 g ($^1/_2$ oz) cup for rice recipe.
2 Follow duck salad recipe steps 1 to 3.
3 Follow rice recipe steps 1 to 3.
4 Follow duck salad recipe step 4.
5 While duck is roasting, follow rice recipe steps 4 to 6.
6 Follow orange and radish salad recipe steps 1 to 5.
7 Follow duck salad recipe steps 5 to 15 and serve with rice and orange and radish salad.

Warm Duck Salad with Mango Chutney

2 whole boneless duck breasts with skin (about 750 g (1½ lb) total weight)
Salt and freshly ground pepper
250 g (8 oz) can sliced water chestnuts
Small bunch scallions
125 g (4 oz) mango chutney
60 g (2 oz) mayonnaise
1 bunch watercress
4 sesame pitta breads
125 g (4 oz) unsalted butter

1 Preheat oven to 240°C (475°F or Mark 9). Place rack in roasting pan.
2 Wash duck breasts under cold running water and dry with paper towels. Using sharp chef's knife or cleaver, halve breasts. Generously season both sides with salt and pepper.
3 Place breasts, skin-side up, on rack and roast 10 minutes.
4 Reduce oven temperature to 230°C (425°F or Mark 8) and roast another 30 minutes.
5 Remove duck from oven and set aside to rest 10 minutes. Reduce oven temperature to 170°C (325°F or Mark 3).
6 Meanwhile, drain water chestnuts; set aside.
7 Wash scallions and dry with paper towels. Trim off ends and discard. Thinly slice 3 scallions; reserve remaining scallions for another use.
8 When duck is cool enough to handle, remove skin. With paring knife, scrape off any remaining fat from duck and skin pieces. Reserve skin.
9 Cut duck into 2.5 cm (1 inch) cubes. Place in medium-size heatproof bowl, cover loosely with foil, and keep warm on top of stove.
10 Using kitchen scissors, cut duck skin into 3 cm (1½ inch) pieces and place on roasting rack. Return pan to oven and roast skin 10 minutes, or until golden brown and crispy.
11 Meanwhile, combine water chestnuts, scallions, chutney, and mayonnaise in large bowl and stir until blended. Add warm duck cubes and stir gently to combine. Cover loosely with foil and keep warm.
12 Wash watercress and dry in a salad spinner or with paper towels. Remove stems and discard. Divide watercress among 4 dinner plates.
13 Using kitchen scissors, cut pitta into triangles and butter insides. Arrange triangles in single layer on baking sheet. Line plate with double thickness of paper towels.
14 Transfer crispy duck skin to paper towels to drain. Place pitta bread in oven to toast about 5 minutes.
15 Top watercress with equal portions of duck mixture. Sprinkle each serving with cracklings and serve with toasted pitta bread.

Rice with Pecans and Mint

500 ml (1 pt) chicken stock
125 g (4 oz) can pecan pieces
175 g (6 oz) long-grain rice
1 juicy orange
15 g (½ oz) minced fresh mint, or 2 teaspoons dried
1 teaspoon salt
1 teaspoon freshly ground pepper

1 In medium-size heavy-gauge saucepan, bring stock to a boil over high heat.
2 While stock is heating, coarsely chop enough pecans to measure 60 g (2 oz); set aside.
3 Add rice to boiling stock and stir. Reduce heat, cover, and simmer gently 12 to 15 minutes, or until rice is tender and liquid has been absorbed.
4 Wash orange and dry with paper towel. Using zester or grater, remove rind, avoiding white pith as much as possible; reserve rind. Squeeze enough juice to measure 4 tablespoons.
5 In medium-size bowl, combine pecans, orange rind and juice, mint, salt. and pepper, and stir with fork; set aside.
6 Fluff rice with fork. Add rice to mixture in bowl and toss gently to combine; set aside at room temperature until ready to serve.

Orange and Radish Salad with Cinnamon Dressing

4 navel oranges
1 bunch radishes
1 lemon
4 tablespoons olive oil
2 teaspoons ground cinnamon
1 to 2 teaspoons sugar (optional)
4 sprigs fresh mint or parsley for garnish (optional)

1 Peel oranges, removing as much white pith as possible. Cut each orange crosswise into thin rounds; set aside.
2 Wash and trim radishes; dry with paper towels. Thinly slice and set aside.
3 Squeeze lemon to measure 2 tablespoons juice.
4 In small bowl, combine oil, lemon juice, cinnamon, and sugar to taste, and beat to combine.
5 Arrange orange and radish slices in alternating rows on 4 salad plates and top with dressing. Garnish each serving with a mint or parsley sprig, if desired. Cover with plastic wrap and set aside until ready to serve.

Meet the Cooks

Bruce Aidells

Early in his cookery career; Californian Bruce Aidells ran an on-campus restaurant at the University of California. He is now a restaurant consultant and teaches Louisiana-style cooking at the California Culinary Academy in San Francisco.

Jane Uetz

Jane Uetz began her cookery career in the test kitchens of a major food company in New York City. She is the director of the consumer and culinary centre of a New York public relations agency. She also teaches cookery classes for business executives.

Mary Carroll Dremann

A professional cook since 1971, Mary Carroll Dremann trained at schools and restaurants in the United States and Europe. In 1983 she opened a retail cookware shop, catering business, and cookery school, all under the name Cuisine Naturelle.

Victoria Wise

Victoria Wise, a self-taught cook, has been cooking professionally since 1971, when she left her graduate studies in philosophy to become the first chef at Berkeley's Chez Panisse, a restaurant well known to US gastronomes. She left Chez Panisse in 1973 to start her own charcuterie, called Pig by the Tail Charcuterie, in Berkeley, California.

Connie Handa Moore

Born in Seattle, Washington, to Japanese immigrants, Connie Handa Moore now lives in New Jersey. She has worked as a caterer, food consultant, cookery teacher, and *sushi* chef. She is the owner of Handa Food Management Inc.

Susan Huberman

Self-taught cook Susan Huberman catered for executive lunches before becoming a freelance food stylist in 1974. Currently she prepares and arranges food for television commercials and print advertising in New York City.

A Wealth of Herbs

Increasingly, herbs are arriving in the markets fresh; the proliferation of health stores and other specialist shops has widened choice, and many cooks with gardens have taken to raising their own. Recent ethnic influences have called attention to once seemingly esoteric herbs. Coriander, for one, is at last gaining deserved popularity in Europe, although cooks in Asia and the Middle East have been using it for centuries.

Anyone wishing to dry fresh herbs can tie them loosely in a bundle and hang them upside down in a cool, dark, well-ventilated place for several weeks. When the leaves are completely dried, strip them from the stems and store them in an airtight container.

Two swifter methods of preserving herbs make use of the microwave oven and the freezer. To microwave herbs, place five or six sprigs at a time between paper towels and microwave them on high for 1 to 3 minutes until the leaves are brittle. Store the leaves loosely in airtight jars.

To freeze herbs, rinse the sprigs and pat them dry. Strip the leaves off the stems and put them into a heavy-duty plastic bag. Gently flatten the bag to force out the air, seal the bag tightly, and place it in your freezer. Use the leaves as the need arises.

Basil (also called sweet basil): This fragrant herb, with its underlying flavour of anise and hint of clove, goes particularly well with tomato.

Chervil: The small, lacy leaves of this herb have a taste akin to parsley with a touch of anise. It is good in salads and salad dressings. Chervil is popular in France where it is often an ingredient in herb mixtures, including *fines herbes*. When used in cooking, chervil should be added at the end, lest its subtle flavour be lost.

Chives: The smallest of the onions, chives grow in grassy clumps. When finely cut, the hollow leaves contribute their delicate, oniony flavour to fresh salads and raw vegetables. Chives should always be used fresh, as dried ones are virtually tasteless.

Coriander (also called cilantro): The serrated leaves of the coriander plant impart a distinctive fragrance and a flavour that is both mildly sweet and bitter. Coriander leaves should be used fresh or added at the end of cooking if their flavour is to be appreciated fully.

Dill: A sprightly herb with feathery leaves, dill enhances cucumber and many other fresh vegetables, as well as fish and shellfish. When used in cooking, dill should be added towards the end of the process to preserve its delicate flavour. Both dill seeds and dill leaves can be